T0231260

Knowledge
Science

**Modeling
the Knowledge
Creation Process**

Knowledge Science

Modeling the Knowledge Creation Process

Edited by
Yoshiteru Nakamori

CRC Press
Taylor & Francis Group
Boca Raton London New York

CRC Press is an imprint of the
Taylor & Francis Group, an **informa** business
A CHAPMAN & HALL BOOK

Contents

Preface

Knowledge science is a problem-oriented interdisciplinary field that takes as its subject modeling of the knowledge creation process and its application and carries out research in disciplines such as knowledge management; management of technology; support for the discovery, synthesis, and creation of knowledge; and innovation theory with the aim of constructing a better knowledge-based society.

Knowledge science develops methodologies and techniques for the management of knowledge and technology; for the discovery, creation, and structuring of knowledge; and for solving organizational and systemic problems. It coordinates various forms of knowledge such as opinions, values or information, science, technology, and diverse standpoints such as industry, academic, government or private sectors. Knowledge science could be established by integrating information science, management science, and systems science.

On the education side, knowledge science produces talented graduates who are capable of comprehensively examining a variety of social issues such as developments in technology, economic–commercial activities, depopulation–aging of society, global warming–depletion of resources, or the stagnation of regional economies, and taking the lead in solving them.

Knowledge engineering (a branch of information science) is mainstream in the world of knowledge science. But knowledge science should aim for integration with knowledge management (for example, human management), the importance of which is recently garnering worldwide attention. However, it will theoretically take some time to integrate the aforementioned three fields and to establish a new academic system. One of the reasonable ways is to attempt their integration in practical use (problem-solving projects), to accumulate actual results, and then to establish them as a discipline in a new field.

Prospective readers of this book are researchers, practitioners, and especially graduate students in the fields of knowledge management, information science, management science, and sociological systems science. The authors of this book are experienced researchers in knowledge science with backgrounds in systems science. Young researchers will find in this book new research themes as well as the importance of knowledge science.

This book introduces six important concepts in knowledge science: (1) knowledge technology, (2) knowledge management, (3) knowledge discovery, (4) knowledge synthesis, (5) knowledge justification, and (6) knowledge construction. Knowledge technology is an umbrella term that includes the previously mentioned concepts as well as knowledge classification, representation and modeling, knowledge identification and acquisition, knowledge searching, knowledge organization, knowledge storage, knowledge conversion, and knowledge dissemination.

Knowledge management are the keywords in knowledge science research. This book introduces the theories and practices of knowledge-oriented management in organizations and covers three different yet related areas: knowledge assets, knowing processes, and knower relations. Knowledge discovery and data mining emerged as a rapidly growing interdisciplinary field that merges databases, statistics, machine learning, and related areas to discover and extract valuable knowledge in large volumes of data.

Knowledge synthesis, knowledge justification, and knowledge construction are quite important when solving real-life problems. This book includes original ideas, such as Oriental systems philosophy, a new episteme in the knowledge-based society and a theory of knowledge construction.

Yoshiteru Nakamori, Editor

About the Authors

Jifa Gu received a B.S.c. from Peking University in China and a Ph.D. from the Institute of Mathematics at the Academy of Sciences of the USSR. He is a professor in the Institute of Systems Science at the Chinese Academy of Sciences, a part-time professor at Dalian University of Science and Technology, and a part-time professor at the graduate school at the Chinese Academy of Sciences; from May 1999 to March 2003 he was a professor at the Japan Advanced Institute of Science and Technology. Beginning in 2005, he has served as the joint director of Shanghai Academy of Systems Science. He has also served as the president of the Systems Engineering Society of China (1994–2002); president (2002–2006) and vice president (2006–2008) of the International Federation for Systems Research; vice president of the International Society of Knowledge and Systems Sciences (2003–2008); and chief editor of *Journal of Systems Science and Systems Engineering* (2003 to present). He has published more than 200 papers and 30 books and has organized several international conferences in the fields of systems engineering, operations research, industrial engineering, and knowledge science. Gu's recent research interests include meta-synthesis methods and system methodology. His current research aims to find methods that may synthesize the data, information, model, knowledge, and the decision maker's judgment and wisdom in solving social and economic system problems using human–machine cooperation. He is also interested in conducting research on system methodology, with a special emphasis on Oriental culture and philosophy. Together with Zhu, Gu proposed the Wuli–Shili–Renli system approach.

Tu Bao Ho is a professor in the School of Knowledge Science at the Japan Advanced Institute of Science and Technology (JAIST). He received a BTech in applied mathematics in October 1978 from Hanoi University of Technology in Vietnam; an M.S. (DEA) in computer science in 1984 from the University of Paris VI in France; a Ph.D. in computer science in February 1987 from the University of Paris VI; and a habilitation in computer science in October 1998 from the University of Paris IX (Dauphine) in France. His research interests include artificial intelligence, conceptual modeling and knowledge-based systems, machine learning, knowledge discovery and data mining, decision science and knowledge-based decision support systems, pattern recognition and intelligent data analysis, computational science, computational medicine, and biology. He has published approximately 50 journal articles, 200 refereed conference papers, and 15 book chapters. He also has edited some conference proceedings.

Yoshiteru Nakamori received a Ph.D. in applied mathematics and physics from Kyoto University in Kyoto, Japan, in 1980. He then served in the Department of Applied Mathematics as faculty of science at Konan University in Kobe, Japan. From September 1984 to December 1985 he stayed at the International Institute for Applied Systems Analysis in Laxenburg, Austria, where he joined the Regional Water Policies Project. He joined the Japan Advanced Institute of Science and Technology in April 1998 as a professor in the School of Knowledge Science. He served as the dean of this school from April 2001 to March 2007. From October 2003 to March 2008 he led a research program on the theory and practice of technology creation based on knowledge science. The goal of this program was to create a world-class center of excellence in (1) theoretical research—with a final target of strategic research and the development of scientific technologies in which knowledge fusion and development in important scientific fields would be studied and then a theory of scientific knowledge creation established; and (2) practical research—as theories were developed, they would be applied in scientific laboratories and approved by feedback from practice. Through repetition of this task, the theory would be improved and the creation of useful scientific technologies promoted. At the same time, graduate students would be trained in this environment and taught to become knowledge coordinators or knowledge creators. Nakamori joined the establishment of the International Society for Knowledge and Systems Sciences in December 2003 and served as president of the society until December 2008.

Zhongtuo Wang is a professor in the School of Management at Dalian University of Technology (DUT), head of the Ph.D. systems engineering program, and the director of the Research Center of Knowledge Science and Technology at DUT. He is a member of the Chinese Academy of Engineering. He was the vice president of the Systems Engineering Society of China. In the 1950s, he joined the Department of Electrical Engineering at Dalian University of Technology. As founder of the Department of Control Engineering at DUT, he contributed greatly to the teaching and research works in the field of optimizing control and computer applications. In 1977, he moved to systems engineering. As one of the originators of the Ph.D. program and research works of systems engineering in China and founder of the Institute of Systems Engineering at DUT, he devoted himself to the task of theoretical research in decision analysis, complex adaptive system, and network optimization. As a leader he has organized a great many projects that apply systems engineering methodologies and techniques to Chinese economic and engineering endeavors, including strategic analysis of regional economic development, production planning of petroleum refineries, planning and scheduling of construction projects, and the impact of information technology on management transformation. He also organized the M.S. and Ph.D. programs in systems engineering and management science at DUT. From 1986 to 1988, he worked at the International Institute for

Applied Systems Analysis (IIASA) in Vienna, Austria, as a research scholar and the head of an international collaborative project and is known internationally for his contributions. He has published 10 books and more than 170 papers and reports. He has received two national awards and nine awards from ministries of Chinese government. He currently works in knowledge management and technological innovation.

Andrzej (Andrew) Piotr Wierzbicki earned an M.E. in telecommunications and control engineering (1960), a Ph.D. in nonlinear dynamics in control (1964), and a D.S.c. in optimization and decision science (1968). He has worked as a professor at Warsaw University of Technology (WUT) (1960–2004); dean of the Faculty of Electronics at WUT (1975–1978); chair of the Systems and Decision Sciences Program at the International Institute for Applied Systems Analysis in Laxenburg, Austria (1979–1984); member of the State Committee for Scientific Research of the Republic of Poland and the chair of its Commission of Applied Research (1991–1994); director general of the National Institute of Telecommunications in Poland (1996–2004); and research professor at the Japan Advanced Institute of Science and Technology in Nomi, Japan (2004–2007). Beside teaching and lecturing for over 45 years and promoting over 100 master's theses and 20 doctoral dissertations at WUT, he has also lectured in doctoral studies at many Polish and international universities. Wierzbicki has authored more than 200 publications, including 14 books, over 80 articles in scientific journals, and over 100 conference papers; he is also the creator of three granted and industrially applied patents. Current interests include vector optimization, multiple criteria and game theory approaches, negotiation and decision support, issues of information society and knowledge civilization, rational evolutionary theory of intuition, theories of knowledge creation and management, knowledge engineering, and modern history of information technology.

Zhichang Zhu's formal education stopped when he was 16 due to China's Cultural Revolution. Without a high school certificate or prior university degree, he obtained a M.S.c. in information management (1990) and a Ph.D. in management systems and sciences (1995), specializing in marketing, and sponsored by British scholarships. Zhu has been a Maoist Red Guard, farm laborer, shop assistant, lorry driver, corporate manager, assistant to the dean of a business school, software engineer, systems analyst, and information systems and information technology business consultant in China, Singapore, Sri Lanka, and England. Zhu is currently a reader in strategy and management at the University of Hull Business School (HUBS). He has held positions as the director of the HUBS Ph.D. program, a visiting research professor in the School of Knowledge Science at the Japan Advanced Institute of Science and Technology, a visiting research professor in strategy and management at South China Normal University, a visiting research professor in International Business Management at International East–West University

(Honolulu and Los Angeles), a visiting lecturing professor in innovation and entrepreneurship at Friedrich Schiller University (Jena, Germany), a visiting lecturing professor in strategy in emerging markets in the East–West Knowledge Leaders Program (Hawaii), and an external examiner for Ph.D. theses for Cape Town University (South Africa) and Swinburne University of Technology (Australia). Zhu has delivered invited keynote speeches and guest lectures to international conferences, universities, and research institutes in China, Germany, Hong Kong, Indonesia, Ireland, Japan, the Gulf, and the United States as well as in the United Kingdom. Zhu is an editor of the international journals *Systems Research and Behavioral Science* and *International Journal of Knowledge and Systems Science*. He is an organizer of the comparative institutional research project sponsored by the Ford Foundation, the international *Systems East & West* project sponsored by the International Federation for Systems Research, the China–Japan–UK research project in systems and knowledge management sponsored by universities and industries in three countries, and a founding member of the International China Association for Management of Technology. Zhu provides business consultancy for Chinese and British corporations in auto-making, leather goods, animal food, and estate industries, including a *Forbes 500* company. Zhu has researched strategy, decision making, marketing theory, information systems, and knowledge management, all from an institutional, comparative perspective, with over 70 articles published in refereed journals, edited books, and international conference proceedings.

1

Introduction

Yoshiteru Nakamori

Japan Advanced Institute of Science and Technology, Japan

CONTENTS

1.1 School of Knowledge Science

The School of Knowledge Science at Japan Advanced Institute of Science and Technology (JAIST*) started in April 1998 and is the first of its kind established in the world to take *knowledge* as a target of science. The school was started after the work of Ikujiro Nonaka, first dean of the school and world renowned for his organizational knowledge creation model (Nonaka and Takeuchi, 1995), in which new knowledge is created between explicit and tacit knowledge through a socialization, externalization, combination, and internalization (SECI) spiral:

1. *Socialization* is a process of sharing experiences and thereby creating tacit knowledge such as shared mental models and technical skills.
2. *Externalization* is a process of articulating tacit knowledge into explicit concepts, taking the shape of metaphors, analogies, concepts, hypotheses, or models.
3. *Combination* is a process of linking explicit knowledge to obtain a knowledge system.
4. *Internalization* is a process of embodying explicit knowledge into tacit knowledge. It is closely related to learning by doing.

---

* JAIST was founded on October 1, 1990, as the first national institute in Japan that consists of graduate schools without undergraduate programs and possesses its own campus and organization for research and education.

1

This theory is revolutionary because it stresses steps leading to knowledge increase definitely, based on the collaboration of a group in knowledge creation and on the rational use of irrational mind capabilities, namely, tacit knowledge, which includes emotions and intuition.

When establishing this school, the founders had to distinguish knowledge from information, which is necessary to explain the structure of the school. Information is knowledge transmitted by, for example, character, sign, or voice or by data arranged to be useful for decision making. Thus, the meaning of *information* can vary from other persons' knowledge to simply collected data. On the other hand, *knowledge* is recognition memorized personally or socially or judgment or a system of judgment that has objective validity. Using the latter definition, people transform data into information and information into knowledge.

The energy that brings about such transformation is called *intelligence*. Intelligence has several meanings, but here we consider computers' ability to judge things automatically or people's ability to understand and learn things. The structure of the school, which includes the following, was constructed in this light:

- *Information science* to develop computers' ability to judge things automatically
- *Management science* to enhance people's ability to understand and learn things

However, knowledge treated in information science is mainly explicit because we have to convey knowledge through computer codes, whereas important knowledge in management science is tacit; it is quite difficult to transfer people's knowledge to others with words. This is the reason we require the third discipline

- *Systems science* to strengthen system's ability by integrating a diversity of knowledge

In the management field, the School of Knowledge Science at JAIST is proud to have pioneered research into knowledge creation theory. Regarding information technology, it has been developing knowledge creation support systems. Systems theory research regarding knowledge integration and creation offers tools and techniques in consultation to business and society. The school integrates these fields at the interdisciplinary project level and facilitates innovation in a variety of fields.

However, at the present stage, knowledge science is more a problem-oriented interdisciplinary academic field than a single discipline. Its mission is to organize and process both objective and subjective information and to create new value, new knowledge. Knowledge science mainly deals with the research areas involving social innovation such as regeneration of organizations, systems, and the mind. However, society's progress is underpinned by technology, and the joint progress of society (needs) and technology (seeds) is essential. Therefore, knowledge science also has the mission to act as a coordinator in extensive technological and social innovations.

To fulfill these missions, the School of Knowledge Science focuses its research and education on observing and modeling the actual process of carrying out the mission, as described in the organizational knowledge creation theory by Nonaka and Takeuchi (1995) or the creative space theory by Wierzbicki and Nakamori (2006), as well as developing methods to carry out the mission. The methods are mainly being developed through the following three areas in the school:

- The application of business science/organizational theories (practical use of tacit knowledge, management of technology, innovation theory)
- The application of information technology/artistic methods (knowledge discovery methods, ways to support creation, knowledge engineering, cognitive science)
- The application of (mathematical) systems theory (systems thinking, the emergence principle, epistemology)

1.2 Approaches to Knowledge Science

We could count several research fields related to knowledge science (Figure 1.1):

- *Knowledge engineering*: Symbolizing (approximating) experts' knowledge to develop artificial intelligence
- *Knowledge discovery*: Mining a large-scale data set to extract partial rules and adding their meanings based on domain knowledge
- *Knowledge construction*: Simulating complex phenomena based on some hypothesis and adding the meanings to emerged properties based on domain knowledge
- *Knowledge management*: Converting distributed (or tacit) knowledge into shared (or explicit) knowledge and using it effectively

The feature of these fields is the use of computers, expanding traditional information science, which means that these fields use subjective knowledge, indicated by italic letters in Figure 1.1.

Organizational knowledge creation is the key academic factor to establish the School of Knowledge Science; after the SECI spiral, some different spirals

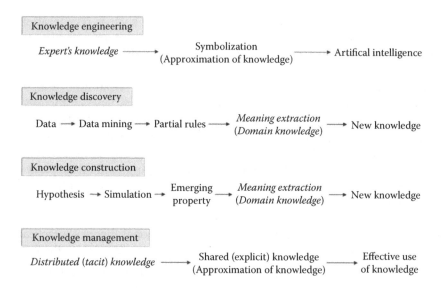

FIGURE 1.1
Existing research fields related to knowledge science.

were proposed. While the SECI spiral is a bottom-up type, Gasson (2004) proposed a top-down type model by analyzing possible transitions among the same four nodes (here group knowledge is called shared knowledge and individual knowledge is called distributed knowledge) in the organizational culture of a Western company. Wierzbicki, Zhu, and Nakamori (2006) proposed personal knowledge creation models that correspond to disciplinary knowledge creation. The feature of these models is to use persons directly, beyond information science (Figure 1.2).

However, to solve complex real-life problems we need knowledge synthesis, collecting, and interpreting different types of knowledge from the cognitive-mental front, scientific-actual front, and social-relational front (Figure 1.3).

Nonaka, Toyama, and Konno (2000) called the dynamic context that is shared and redefined in the knowledge creation process *ba*, which refers not just to a physical space but also includes virtual spaces based on the Internet, for instance, and more mental spaces that involve sharing experiences and ideas. They stated that knowledge is not something that can exist independently; it can exist only in a form embedded in ba, which acts as a context that is constantly shared by people.

From the hypothesis that knowledge science will be established at the ba where several disciplines are integrated, we should expand our research into social and technological innovation to foster revitalization projects and collaborative projects with enterprises. For example, suppose that a student participates in a regional environmental project of a certain city. If the main theme is the extent of reductions in the concentration of carbon dioxide and

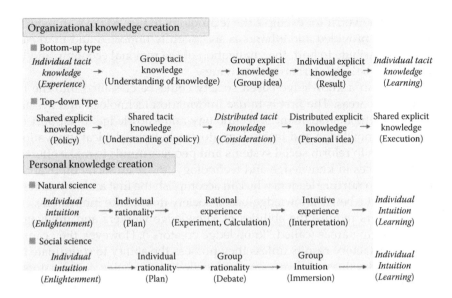

FIGURE 1.2
Organizational or personal knowledge creation models.

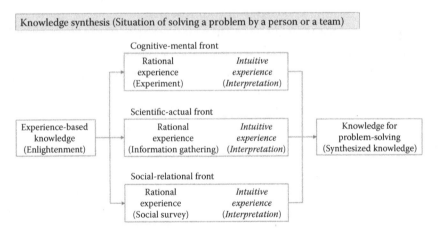

FIGURE 1.3
Knowledge synthesis to solve complex real-life problems.

the analysis of economic effects and the secondary theme is converting food residue into ethanol, the student would receive guidance from the School of Materials Science for the secondary theme. In addition, the qualities of a coordinator should be required such as in requesting assistance from the public to further the project, mediating between the parties concerned, and collating and providing data and opinions. In such a case we will request the municipal representative to act as a mentor and to contribute to the student's growth. Moreover, if for example the technology to turn Malaysian palm oil to ethanol is provided and ethanol is successfully imported and marketed, this will contribute to both the vitalization of the regional economy and the student's growth in international activities.

Our tasks in a knowledge-based society could be classified into the following three areas. The first is to use information technology and systems science and the management of technology and knowledge to support the creation of knowledge and technology (to create technological innovation). The second is to reform social systems and people's minds to make effective use of advances in knowledge and technology (to create social innovation). The third is to nurture leaders who can accomplish the first and second tasks and construct a better knowledge-based society (to nurture innovators).

Such leaders require the abilities of knowledge workers and innovators in wide-ranging areas (called "knowledge creators"). However, they cannot achieve satisfactory results unless they possess the ability to coordinate the opinions and values of diverse people (called "knowledge coordinators"). Accordingly, we should aim to promote cutting-edge research and education into the theory and practices of social and technological innovation.

Consider the following questions while reading this book:

1. Are you treating knowledge in your research?
    a. If yes, what kind of knowledge are you treating?
    b. (Note) You might treat just information, not knowledge.
    c. (Note) There is a critique that one can manage information but cannot manage knowledge.
2. Try to understand what ba is (ba = creative environment).
    a. What kind of ba are you involved in?
    b. (Note) It is said that knowledge can exist only in a form embedded in ba.
    c. (Note) This definition of knowledge is significant when considering its difference from information.
3. Do you think that you are creating knowledge?
    a. If yes, explain your spiral in creating knowledge.
    b. (Note) You can either consider your individual study or your research in your group.
    c. (Note) Remember the definition of knowledge, which is not just information or data.
4. Do you have a confidence that you will become an innovator or a knowledge coordinator?
    a. If yes, explain your style of study to become an innovator or a coordinator.

b. (Note) An innovator should have knowledge in wide-ranging areas.

c. (Note) A coordinator should manage knowledge in wide-ranging areas.

1.3 Contents of the Book

In Chapter 2, "Knowledge Technology," Zhongtuo Wang, from the School of Management at Dalian University of Technology in China, describes knowledge technology, which can be understood as a new emerging discipline applying the outcome of principles of knowledge science to knowledge processing, knowledge management, and knowledge creation. Considering the important role of systems science in providing methodology and techniques for organization and management of human endeavors, the author proposes to establish a new branch of systems engineering called "knowledge systems engineering" for a new approach to knowledge processing and knowledge management, which differs from "knowledge engineering" in artificial intelligence at its area of study not only limited to the technological aspect but also concerned with organizational and cognitive aspects. After discussing the architecture of knowledge systems, the author describes definitions and roles of many concepts related to knowledge technology such as the knowledge-gathering and -capturing technology and systems, including the technologies and tools as databases and text bases, data warehouse and data marts, web technologies, cloud computing, knowledge repositories, knowledge portals, search engines, intelligent agents, and knowledge maps. For the system support of knowledge discovery and creation, the author describes both the discovery of explicit knowledge and technological aid for idea generation and some knowledge-sharing technology and systems like lesson learned system, expertise-locator system, and community of practices. For the knowledge application system, the author describes some mechanisms and technologies, including the help desk, fault diagnosis systems, expert systems, as well as decision support systems.

In Chapter 3, "Knowledge Management," Zhichang Zhu, from the University of Hull Business School in the United Kingdom, considers this topic from a systems-theoretic point of view. First the author answers to the questions: Why has knowledge management considerably promoted recent years? What is knowledge, and is it manageable? Then, the author takes a pragmatic approach to knowledge-based management that gears managerial efforts and organization resources to the following: get the knowledge vision right, focus on organizational management, and make it work in particular contexts. Adopting a pragmatist and holistic perspective, the author introduces readers to the theories and practices of knowledge-oriented management in organizations, which covers purposeful coping of three differentiated yet related areas: knowledge assets, knowing processes, and knower relations. The author also suggests that a systems approach promoting synergy among efficiency, creativity, and legitimacy will increase opportunities for organizations in the search for competitive advantage and sustainable prosperity. This chapter itself is a conscious attempt in bridging systems and knowledge sciences with an explicit focus on enhancing organizational management practice.

Chapter 4, "Knowledge Discovery," by Tu Bao Ho of the School of Knowledge Science at Japan Advanced Institute of Science and Technology, discusses how knowledge discovery and data mining (KDD) emerged as a rapidly growing interdisciplinary field that merges together databases, statistics, machine learning, and related areas to discover and extract valuable knowledge in large volumes of data. The knowledge discovery addressed in this chapter is an information science ingredient of knowledge science, which is essentially the finding or discovering knowledge in data. It is an interdisciplinary field, having roots in the new field of knowledge discovery and data mining in the last two decades. Almost all organizations have collected huge amounts of data in their databases. These organizations need to understand their data or to discover useful knowledge as patterns or models from their data. Meeting this increasing need in the digitalized society, KDD has been becoming an attractive science and technology in both theory and practice. The author provides basic concepts and methods of KDD as well as its typical applications and begins with an overview of data, information, and knowledge. Then, definitions of *knowledge discovery* and *data mining* are provided, followed by the steps in the KDD process. The main part of the chapter covers the essential ideas of typical KDD methods and the challenges and trends of KDD after its 15 years of development. Finally, text mining—a typical branch of KDD—and its application are briefly introduced.

In Chapter 5, "Knowledge Synthesis," by Jifa Gu of the Institute of Systems Science at the Chinese Academy of Sciences in China, the author discusses that the most common knowledge can be recognized by the majority of people. However, due to the methods of getting data, information, and knowledge from different sources or inferring knowledge by using different mechanisms, under most circumstances, people will use different kinds of knowledge to express their own thoughts at first and through discussing and even debating with others may use synthesis to reach consensus. It means that some knowledge can be recognized only through the synthesis of thoughts. Then, during implementation, in which people put the knowledge into practice, they have to use synthesis of actions. The author first introduces various definitions of knowledge synthesis, and then several existing approaches to knowledge synthesis. Among them, the author's original works are the meta-synthesis system, which is useful for synthesis of thoughts; and the Wuli-Shili-Renli system, which is useful for synthesis of actions. The author also introduces expert mining, which helps to dig deep thoughts from individual experts or a group of experts. Finally, the author provides some case studies in the fields of economic, social, and human body systems.

Chapter 6, "Knowledge Justification," by Andrzej Wierzbicki of the Poland National Institute of Telecommunication, presents another perspective of viewing knowledge technology and science: *How does knowledge evolve? How do we justify knowledge, that is, check whether new knowledge is correct and useful? What is specific in knowledge justification in the new era after informational revolution?* The author starts with what is "today" in the beginnings of the era of knowledge society; then turns to what we mean by "knowledge" and "episteme," the way of creating and justifying knowledge characteristic for a given era or cultural sphere. The author discusses the naturally circular, positive feedback type of knowledge creation and justification processes that, contrary to a tradition in philosophy, are not a paradox but are natural evolutionary phenomena. The author shows how we should look today at the processes of knowledge creation and what are accepted methods of justifying knowledge. Finally, the author presents diverse spirals of knowledge creation and discusses the principles of developing a new episteme of the era of knowledge civilization.

Finally, Chapter 7, "Knowledge Construction," by Yoshiteru Nakamori of the School of Knowledge Science at Japan Advanced Institute of Science and Technology, considers the problem of knowledge construction and proposes a theory of knowledge construction systems, which consists of three fundamental parts: a knowledge construction system; a structure–agency–action paradigm; and evolutionary constructive objectivism. The first is a model of collecting and synthesizing knowledge; the second relates to necessary abilities of actors when collecting knowledge in individual domains; and the third comprises a set of principles to justify collected and synthesized knowledge. The author starts with a brief introduction of a basic systems approach called "informed systems thinking", followed by a summary of the theory of knowledge construction systems. The author then explains its three fundamental parts with an explanation of characters of the theory. Finally, the author concludes that we should nurture talented people, called "knowledge coordinators". How can we nurture such people? One of the answers is that we should establish knowledge science, educate young students by this discipline, and encourage learning by doing.

2

Knowledge Technology

Zhongtuo Wang

Dalian University of Technology

CONTENTS

This is an introductory chapter to knowledge technology. The chapter first introduces knowledge technology as a soft technology and its relations with knowledge science and then suggests that the knowledge systems engineering (KSE) as a new approach to knowledge processing and knowledge management technology. From a process-oriented view, the chapter introduces and analyzes the systems and mechanisms of knowledge management. It also introduces the knowledge-gathering and -capturing technology and systems, including the technologies and tools as databases and text bases, data warehouse and data marts, web technologies, cloud computing, knowledge repositories, knowledge portals, search engines, intelligent agents, and knowledge maps. For the system support of knowledge discovery and creation, it briefly describes both the discovery of explicit knowledge and technological aid for idea generation and some knowledge-sharing technology and systems like lesson-learned system, expertise-locator system, and community of practices. For the knowledge application system, it describes some mechanisms and technologies, including the help desk, fault diagnosis systems, expert systems, as well as decision support systems.

2.1   Knowledge Science and Knowledge Technology

2.1.1   Introduction

We are living in a new emerging era of knowledge economy. This new kind of economy can be explained as follows: "Knowledge-driven economy is one in which the generation and exploitation of knowledge play the predominant part in the creation of wealth" (United Kingdom, Department of Trade and Industry, 1998). The new economy is becoming a reality for many developed countries.

In the agricultural economy, hundreds even thousand years before, the key factor of production was land. Later in the industrial economy, the main factors of production were labor and capital. Now, in the knowledge economy, the main factors are information and knowledge.

The transformation from the old economy to a new is driven by the rise of knowledge intensity in economy and knowledge-based innovation. The recognition of technology as the key competitive advantage leads people to pay more attention to knowledge workers. Now the percentage of blue collar workers in the labor force is decreasing and the percentage of information and knowledge workers is increasing. The role of technology and innovation are also observed in the service industry. In recent years the corporations in developed countries moved their manufacturing works (with low profits) to developing countries and kept the knowledge-intensive works (with high profits like R&D; services) in the homeland.

This is a great challenge to developing countries. China is a typical example. In recent years, the Chinese economy grew rapidly. But now the economy confronts with some constraints for the further development. One of the constraints is a lack of core technology. Chinese firms must pay for the technology imported and pay more resource/environment costs only to get little from the labor. Shortage of natural resources becomes another constraint for sustainable development, and low level of production leads to overconsumption of resources.

In order to overcome these difficulties, the Chinese government takes measures to promote knowledge innovation and technology innovation and hopes China will be "an innovation-oriented country" by 2020. Some institutions of knowledge science and technology innovation have been organized. The post-graduate programs around knowledge science and innovation have been set up. Researchers in these fields are working in different aspects of knowledge processing and knowledge management. This will help China catch up in world development.

2.1.2 Hard and Soft Technology

In order to promote the development of knowledge application, we need not only scientific ideas and methodology of knowledge processing and knowledge management, but also some technology to realize these activities.

Technology plays an ever-increasing role in the development of the economy. For a long time, people used the word *technology* to refer to the application of rules, methods, and tools of natural science to solve problems in the material world. This implies the products and the processes are visible or tangible. This is because in the age of industrial economy, material production plays the dominant role.

In recent years, the concepts of soft science and soft technology have been introduced by scholars of interdisciplinary research. Traditional science (mainly natural science and engineering) in many cases has been called *hard science* and traditional technology (based on natural science) is called *hard technology*. In an earlier period, there were different understandings of the soft technology. Some scholars thought the term "soft" implied that the method and tools were not very rigorous or accurate (when compared with the hard science), no matter what area the technology is applied. The emphasis is on the means. Other scholars think "soft" implies that people apply such technology for mental works and not for material processing, no matter what kind of methods and tools come from. The emphasis is on the purpose.

At the same time, some Eastern scholars began to investigate the definition and contents of soft technology. Zhouying Jin, a pioneer of soft technology, introduced some definitions of this new kind of technology in her paper (Jin, 2002). In the 1970s, Japanese scholars proposed the concepts of *soft science* and *soft series of science and technology* (NISTEP, 1988, 1989). These are the concepts in opposition to the traditional concepts of *hard science* and *hard technology*, based on natural science and engineering. In a report by the Soft Series Science and Technology Investigation Committee (1990) the definition of *soft series of science and technology* was revised as follows (Jin, 2002, p. 10):

> It is a new science and technology area, in which the aim (sciences) is to clarify the mechanism of human knowledge activities such as cognition, thinking, consequence, judgment, and innovation as well as their behavior; to deal with and operate those tools that are supporting or partially substituting above activities and those information and knowledge that is generated by activities (technology).

This report also declared that technology could be classified as both hardware and "human ware."

Soft technology has been studied more in detail in Jin's book (Jin, 2005). She describes soft technology as "operable knowledge systems derived from social sciences, non-natural sciences and non-scientific (traditional) knowledge aimed at solving various practical problems."

All these definitions cover wide areas and may not be accepted by people with natural science backgrounds, but this new discipline will put the skills and experiences in service and social activities on the scientific basis and promote the development of interdisciplinary areas.

Soft technology must have two features (Jin 2002):

1. it should be an operable knowledge system of means, tools, and rules for the solution of problems; and

2. it should aim at practice for providing the service of social change and economic development.

The most challenging area in soft technology is intelligent and knowledge-intensive service. It is closely related to innovation. People often consider that soft technology mainly serves innovation. But there are more application areas.

Jin's book lists some commercial technologies as soft technology: Accounting technology, logistic technology, modern management technology, public relations technology, advertisement technology, insurance technology, and purchasing technology.

Even in material production, people cannot rely on hard technology itself to turn out products or acquire market shares. "Many other functions are needed for technology to be injected and infused into products and services" (Jin, 2002). We must have correct strategies, collect the necessary funds, design products based on new technology that can be adopted by society, and build up marketing procedures.

For the sake of their continuous survival, enterprises need not only invent their new products and readjust the technology structure by technology innovation, but also address issues involving business planning, purchasing, acquisition, and foreign investments to remain competitive. The means by which all these can be done efficiently is itself a soft technology. Jin (2005) considers standardization, processing, and regularization of these processes to be examples of soft technology.

Human society has developed different kinds of business rules and financial tools that suit different cultures, social systems, and technology levels. Those processes of applying creative thoughts and ideas in production, marketing, and profit-making have, over time, become standardized, regularized, and formalized into mechanisms, rules, or systems. This process of human creative activity belongs to soft technology. These technologies are similar to natural science technologies, but they are accumulated from experiences and formed after thousands of "tests" and experiments (in this experiment, the laboratory is human society).

2.1.3 Knowledge Science and Knowledge Technology

As defined in Chapter 1, *knowledge science* is a problem-oriented interdisciplinary field that takes as its subject the modeling of the knowledge creation process and its application, and carries out research in such disciplines as knowledge management, management of technology, support for the discovery, synthesis and creation of knowledge, and innovation theory with the aim of constructing a better knowledge-based society.

Knowledge technology can be understood as a new emerging discipline applying the outcome of principles of knowledge science to knowledge processing, knowledge management, and knowledge creation.

According to the reports of Japan mentioned above, knowledge science and technology belongs to soft science and technology by the following reasons:

1. They belong to "new science and technology area." The investigations of knowledge and its roles have a long history, but the disciplines of knowledge science, technology, and engineering emerged only in the later years of past century.

2. It is self-evident that their aim is to clarify the mechanism of human knowledge activities such as cognition, thinking, consequence, judgment, and innovation as well as their behaviors.

3. They deal with and operate those tools that are supporting knowledge-intensive activities, and information and knowledge generated by these activities.

4. Some tools of hard science and technology are often used in the implementation of knowledge technology, but the main ideas and methodology are from the soft aspects.

In knowledge technology, not only the pure technical methods and tools are invented but also the methods and tools of knowledge management and knowledge enabling are invented and implemented.

Since knowledge technology is established "through the conscious use of those common laws or experiences in economic, social, and humanistic activities, and then shapes rules, mechanisms, means, institutions, methods, and procedures which contribute to the improvement, adaptation, or control of the subjective and the objective world" (Jin, 2005), so it belongs to the category of soft technology.

2.2 Knowledge Systems and Knowledge Systems Engineering

2.2.1 Knowledge Systems

In this section the system view of knowledge processing and knowledge management are introduced. In these systems, the components include knowledge workers, knowledge processing tools (software), knowledge networks, and man–machine interface devices (hardware). All these components have physical (visible) or organizational (invisible) connections.

The generation and exploitation of knowledge contains a series of knowledge processing cycles including the capture, analysis, creation, and application of knowledge within an organization. It also relates to problems of searching and finding useful information, but the most important is the creation of new knowledge.

Some of these processes are realized by given kinds of technological systems and tools. These systems constitute the knowledge-processing system. All the processes and systems must be organized and managed and the functions of organization and management are realized by the knowledge management system.

Knowledge management has received a lot of attention, not only in practitioner and scholarly literature, but also in professional services, companies, and in business organizations of all industrial sectors. The core issue of knowledge management is to place knowledge under guidance in order to get value from it. The definition and contents of knowledge management will be introduced in Chapter 3 of this book.

The field of knowledge management has drawn insights, ideas, theories, metaphors, and approaches from diverse disciplines including organizational science and human resource management, computer science and information system, management science, and psychology and sociology, among others.

In recent years, there are two approaches to the knowledge management, the first one put the focus on information management since information is the carrier of knowledge. The main task is supplying existing knowledge (mainly explicit) to knowledge workers. This approach can be easily connected to the knowledge-processing system, and sometimes they can be integrated into a total system. The second one put the focus on human resource management, since the knowledge (especially tacit) is stored and created in human brain. The main task is how to organize people to join the knowledge work.

Since knowledge management and knowledge creation are complex tasks, each of the above approaches has its own limitations and we must have a systems point of view to integrate these two approaches into a unified framework.

Moreover, the concept knowledge management itself cannot fully describe all the knowledge activities. In fact, the term *management* implies control and constraint, but knowledge (especially in the human brain) is inherently uncontrollable. The important thing is learning how to enable knowledge to promote development of human endeavor. So the concept of knowledge enabling or knowledge facilitating is more appropriate for understanding the role of knowledge in real life.

2.2.2 Knowledge Systems Engineering

Systems science has an important role to play in providing methodology and techniques for organization and management of human endeavors, including knowledge management.

Systems engineering is the technological discipline of organization and management of systems. In 50 years, since the founding of this interdisciplinary area, it has many successful applications. Based on the systems engineering thinking and methodology, some interdisciplinary problems can be solved satisfactorily. In the area of energy industry, *Energy Systems Engineering* investigates the energy exploration, transmission and utilization problems from a unified and systemic view, no matter what kind of the resource and end-user are. *Information Systems Engineering* investigates the information creation—processing, transmission, and utilization—in a unified and systemic view, no matter the information, are in a telecommunication system, computer network, or biotechnological system.

Every discipline and every profession will become increasingly more involved with knowledge. This universality presents major problems in the management of knowledge. Why not investigate the knowledge acquisition, manipulation, dissemination, and creation from a unified and systemic view? From this point of view, the author of this chapter has suggested to establish a new branch of systems engineering: *Knowledge systems engineering* (Wang, 2004). It can be defined as the discipline of organization and management of knowledge systems.

It differs from the knowledge engineering in artificial intelligence at its area of study not only limited to the technological aspect but also concerned with organizational and cognitive aspects. Also from the dimensions of study it differs from traditional human resource management and information management. Both the technological and human-behavior elements are covered in a unified framework.

Knowledge systems engineering as an application-oriented discipline integrates both the technology-centered and human-centered approaches, integrates knowledge management and knowledge enabling. Another advantage of the system engineering approach is that the knowledge-processing system and knowledge-management system are interwoven together and can be studied in unified modeling by a systems engineering approach. Such an approach may be more acceptable by people with experience in both science-technology and humanities.

The knowledge system is a man–machine system in which human factors play an important role. *Knowledge Systems Engineering* will adopt a top-down approach to study how to realize the system functions and a bottom-up approach to investigate characteristics of each component as well as their interrelations. The knowledge system is a complex system with high abstractness. In order to build up a framework of knowledge systems engineering, we will start to set up the architecture of knowledge systems (Wang, 2004).

2.2.3   Architecture of Knowledge Systems

Some people think of knowledge as a thing or object owned by somebody. Thinking of knowledge as an object will lead people to focus on databases and other storage devices; on identifying, organizing, and collecting knowledge. Of course, they must be measurable. Knowledge objects need to be maintained and retired.

Another way of thinking of knowledge is as a process. The process perspective brings a very different focus to the domain of knowledge, focusing more on dynamic aspects of knowledge, such as sharing, creating, adapting, learning, applying, and communicating.

Both of these ways of thinking about knowledge are useful for understanding different attributes of knowledge. The question of whether knowledge is a thing or a process is like the wave–particle duality in quantum physics. There are two equally valid experimental processes regarding the properties of light.

System architecture can be used to represent the structural characteristics and modular composition from a certain facet. It does not describe the technical details. System architecture is more object-oriented. Architecture of knowledge systems consist of

1. organization architecture
2. personnel architecture
3. technological architecture
4. business architecture
5. cultural architecture

The discussion of these architectures in detail can be found in Wang (2004). In the next section the technological architecture and knowledge processes will be analyzed.

2.3   Knowledge Management Service and Systems

2.3.1   Knowledge Management Systems

An integrated knowledge system consists of two component systems: knowledge processing system and knowledge management system. Computer aided design (CAD) systems and computer aided manufacturing (CAM) systems are typical knowledge processing systems. The knowledge management system can be defined in a broad or narrow sense. In the broad sense, it includes not only technological components but also knowledge workers and their social relations. In the narrow sense, according to Maier (2007), the knowledge management system is defined as follows:

A knowledge management system (KMS) is an ICT system in the sense of an application system or an ICT platform that combines and integrates functions for the contextualized handling of both explicit and tacit knowledge, throughout the organization or that part of the organization that is targeted by a KM initiative. A KMS offers integrated services to deploy KM instruments for networks of participants, i.e., active knowledge workers, in knowledge-intensive business processes along the entire knowledge life cycle. Ultimate aim of KMS is to support the dynamics of organizational learning and organizational effectiveness.

2.3.2   Knowledge Management Service

As shown in the above definition, the knowledge management system offers knowledge management service to knowledge workers. A service in general is an abstract resource that represents a capability of performing tasks that form a coherent functionality from the point of view of provider entities. Knowledge management services are a subset of services offered in an organization, both basic and composed, whose functionality supports high-level knowledge management instruments as part of on-demand knowledge management initiatives (Maier, 2007). Examples for these services are:

- find expert
- submit experience
- publish skill profile
- revisit learning resource
- join community-of-interest

Services are provided by service providers that procure the service implementations, supply their service descriptions, and provide the necessary support.

Knowledge management services often provide a solution to a defined business problem to special needs of one or a small number of organizational units. Basic services can be composed into new composite services enabling large integrated knowledge management services.

2.3.3　Knowledge Management Service Infrastructure

Knowledge management service infrastructure contains three layers (Maier and Remus, 2007).

1. Conceptual layer: Defines which services are required in every core business, which services are offered by which service processes, who is responsible for them and what resources are allocated to fulfill them. Models that support the conceptual layer should be developed as part of a knowledge management project.

2. Information and communication technology layer: Defines the services offered by heterogeneous application systems that have to be selected and combined in order to provide basic knowledge management services. A comprehensive platform type solution for these services has been termed enterprise knowledge infrastructure. Services can be structured into the following categories:
   a. Infrastructure services
   b. Integration services
   c. Knowledge services
   d. Personalization services
   e. Access services

3. Knowledge management service layer: The main task of this layer is to bridge the gap between the conceptual layer and the information and communication layer. Knowledge services have to be composed using services offered by heterogeneous application systems from the information and communication layer. It must support the

discovery, call, and provision of knowledge services from different activities of business processes.

2.3.4 Technological Infrastructure

The technical implementation of the system is based on the corporate intranet and the Internet. An integrated technological infrastructure contains the following layers in bottom-up order (Applehans et al., 1999):

1. The repositories constitute the lowest layer. It is the knowledge and information sources, and contains the data warehouses, legacy systems, document repositories, and public folders.
2. Transportation layer corresponds to an intranet infrastructure, extended by collaboration and streaming media tools.
3. Application layer includes calendars, yellow pages, tools for analysis, etc.
4. Intelligence layer consists of search, personalization, and agent technologies.
5. Access layer stresses security technologies, including firewall, authentication, etc.
6. User interface, mainly a web browser.

2.4 Knowledge Processes

2.4.1 Knowledge Processes in Problem Solving and Innovation

From the process-oriented view, the knowledge activities in organization (e.g., enterprise) are organized in different stages; each stage is composed of knowledge processes.

There are four kinds of knowledge processes in the innovation or complex problem solving, including the processes through which knowledge is gathered, organized, captured, discovered or created, shared and applied. These four kinds of processes are supported by a set of seven knowledge subprocesses (Becerra-Fernandez, Gonzalez, and Sabherwal, 2004). Four of them are related to Nonaka (1994). These four subprocesses are focusing on the ways in which knowledge is converted through interaction between tacit and explicit knowledge: socialization, externalization, internalization, and combination. The other three subprocesses—exchange, direction, and routines—are based on Grant (1996a, 1996b) and Nahapiet and Ghoshal (1998).

2.4.2   Knowledge Gathering and Capture

Knowledge gathering can be defined as the process of acquiring either explicit or tacit knowledge that resides within people, artifacts, or organizational entities. Moreover, the knowledge may be gathered from outside the organizational boundaries, including suppliers, customers, consultants, prior employers of the organization's new employees, and even the competitors.

Knowledge can come in a variety of forms: structured, semi-structured, or unstructured. They can be gathered by manual, semi-automatic, or automatic acquiring systems, and by working out a way to group, index, or categorize them in some way.

Some parts of the existing knowledge may be codified or documented as explicit knowledge, and other parts reside in peoples' minds as tacit knowledge. People identify what they need and organize the explicit parts for the convenience of direct application and further processing.

Knowledge capture process contains two subprocesses: externalization and internalization. Externalization process converts tacit knowledge into explicit forms such as words, concepts, visuals, or figurative language (for instance, metaphors, analogies, and narratives). It translates individuals' tacit knowledge into explicit forms that can be more easily understood by other persons in the group. This is a difficult process because tacit knowledge is often hard to articulate. As suggested by Nonaka (1994), one way the externalization may be accomplished is through the use of metaphor (for example, understanding and experiencing one kind of thing in terms of another). A typical example of externalization is a consultant team writing a document that describes the lessons the team has learned about the client organization, client executives, and approaches that work in such an assignment. By this way the tacit knowledge acquired by the team members is captured.

Internalization converts the explicit knowledge into tacit knowledge. It represents the traditional notion of "learning." The explicit knowledge may be embodied in action and practice, so that the individual acquiring knowledge can reexperience what others have gone through.

Knowledge gathered and captured must be stored in knowledge repository. In building organizational knowledge repositories, a number of technologies including databases, text bases, data warehouses, and data marts can be used.

2.4.3   Knowledge Discovery and Creation

Knowledge discovery can be defined as the development of new tacit or explicit knowledge from data and information, or from the synthesis of prior knowledge. The discovery of new explicit knowledge relies most directly on combination, and the discovery of new tacit knowledge relies mostly on socialization.

New explicit knowledge can be discovered through combination. Multiple bodies of explicit knowledge, data, and information are integrated to create more complex sets of explicit knowledge. Through communication, integration, and systemization of multiple streams of explicit knowledge, new explicit knowledge is created—either incrementally or radically (Nahapiet and Ghoshal, 1998). Existing explicit knowledge, data, and information are reconfigured, recategorized, and recontextualized to produce new explicit knowledge. Data and text mining techniques may be used to uncover new relationships among explicit data and text, and may lead to predictive or categorization models that create new knowledge.

As for the tacit knowledge, the integration of multiple streams for the creation of new knowledge occurs through the mechanism of socialization (Nonaka, 1994). Socialization is the synthesis of tacit knowledge across individuals, usually through joint activities instead of written or verbal instructions. A good example is how apprenticeships help newcomers to see how other people think by transferring ideas and images. Storytelling is also an effective tool.

The knowledge creation process by individual knowledge worker includes the experience, nurtured, enlightenment, and sublimated stages. Once when a new idea is created, the worker will organize and externalize it.

2.4.4 Knowledge Sharing and Exchange

Knowledge sharing can be defined as the transfer process through which explicit and tacit knowledge are communicated to other individuals. Knowledge sharing needs an effective transfer so that the recipient of knowledge can understand it well enough to act upon it. The sharing of knowledge may take place across individuals and groups, departments, or organizations. It is an important process in enhancing organizational innovativeness and performance.

The socialization process is used to tacit knowledge sharing. It facilitates the sharing in cases both the new tacit knowledge is created as well as when new tacit knowledge is not created.

The *exchange process* is used to explicit knowledge sharing. This kind of process can be used to communicate or transfer explicit knowledge between individuals, groups, and organizations. In fact, the process of exchange of explicit knowledge does not differ from the process through which information is communicated. A typical example of exchange is a product design manual transferred from one employee to another who can use the explicit knowledge contained.

2.4.5 Knowledge Integration and Application

Knowledge from different sources with different attributes must be integrated to meet the requirement of problem solving. The knowledge application process is used to make decisions, to facilitate innovation, and to perform tasks. The success of knowledge application depends on available knowledge, and the latter depends on the processes of knowledge capture, discovery, and storage.

In applying knowledge, some people who make use of it do not necessarily need to comprehend it. All that is needed is how the knowledge is used to guide actions. Therefore the knowledge utilization benefits from two processes that do not involve the actual transfer or exchange of knowledge between the concerned individuals. These two processes are directions and routines.

Direction refers to the process through which individuals possessing the knowledge direct the action of another individual without transferring to that person the knowledge underlying the direction. This preserves the advantages of specialization and avoids the difficulties inherent in the transfer of tacit knowledge. An example is when a production worker calls experts to ask them how to solve a particular problem with a machine, then proceeds to solve the problem based on the instructions given by the experts. This production worker does so without acquiring the experts' knowledge in detail. Next time the worker faces a similar problem, she would be unable to identify it as such and would be unable to solve it without calling experts. The difference between the direction and socialization or exchange is, in the latter case, the knowledge is actually internalized by other persons.

Routines involve the utilization of knowledge embedded in procedures, rules, and norms that guide future behavior. Routines economize on communication more than directions because they are embedded in procedures or technologies (e.g., software). However, they take time to develop and rely on constant repetition. An inventory management system utilizes considerable knowledge about the relationship between demand and supply, but neither the knowledge nor the directions are communicated through individuals.

2.4.6   Knowledge Management Mechanism

In order to realize these knowledge processes, the knowledge management mechanisms must be used. Knowledge management mechanisms are organizational or structural means to promote knowledge management. They may utilize technology and may not, but they do involve some kind of organizational arrangement or social means of facilitating knowledge management.

Examples of knowledge management mechanisms include

- Analogies and metaphors
- Brain storming
- Learning by doing
- On-the-job training
- Learning by observation
- Telephone conversations

- Memos, manuals, letters
- Face-to-face meetings

Examples of knowledge management technologies include

- Webpage retrieving
- Web-based discussion groups
- Repositories of best practice
- Case-based reasoning
- Groupware
- Computer supported collaborative work

More long-term knowledge management mechanisms include hiring a chief knowledge officer, cooperative projects across departments, traditional hierarchical relationships, and employee rotation across departments.

Knowledge management systems utilize a variety of knowledge management mechanisms and technologies to support the knowledge management processes. Depending on the knowledge processes listed above, comprehensive knowledge management systems can be classified into several kinds: knowledge gathering and capture systems, knowledge discovery systems, knowledge sharing systems, and knowledge application systems. In the following sections, all the systems and their mechanisms and technologies are described. Contents are mainly from Becerra-Fernandez, Gonzalez, and Sabherwal (2004) and Maier (2007).

2.5   Knowledge Gathering and Capture Technology and Systems

One of the important objectives of knowledge management is to gather, codify, organize, and store relevant information for later use by organizational members.

2.5.1   Knowledge Gathering Technology and Systems

Knowledge gathering systems support the process of acquiring and eliciting either explicit or tacit knowledge that may reside in people, artifacts, or organizational entities. Such kinds of systems can help capture knowledge existing either within or outside organizational boundaries, among employees, consultants, customers, suppliers, and even competitors as well as employers of the organization's new employees.

The knowledge gathering systems use the following technologies to build the organizational repositories (Standard Australia, 2002):

1. *Databases and text bases*: Electronic data generated by daily transactions are usually recorded in business documents and notes or in transaction records. Knowledge is stored in structured database systems and constitutes a part of the organizational memory. In addition to data and text, multimedia systems organize and make available to users their knowledge assets in a variety of other representational forms, including images, audio, and video formats.

2. *Data warehouses and data marts*: Unlike organizational databases that typically store current data related to specific business functions, a data warehouse stores data that retains historical and cross-functional perspectives. Data are extracted daily from the business transaction systems and from any other systems deemed relevant. Compared to data warehouses, which combined databases across an entire enterprise, data marts are usually smaller and focus on a particular subject or department.

3. *Web technologies*: The Internet and web technologies provide virtually unlimited storage as part of huge server farms that may be located all around the world. The Internet can link workers to mountains of digital records stored on the web all over the world with blinding speed. The Internet benefits the users by reducing communication costs, enhancing communication, accelerating the distributing of knowledge, and facilitating service delivery. The World Wide Web (WWW) is a universally accepted set of standards for storing, retrieving, formatting, and displaying information in a networked environment. It makes available to the requesting public, knowledge artifacts in the form of documents, files, photos, drawings, videos, sound, and other various holders of knowledge. Knowledge artifacts are stored and displayed on the web in the form of webpages. Web pages are hypermedia documents that often express the content in an artistic and dynamic fashion using stylish typography, colorful graphics, push-button interactivity, and sound and video. These pages can be linked electronically to other pages regardless of where they are located and can be viewed by any type of computer, including mobile phones.

4. *Cloud computing*: Cloud computing is a way of computing via the Internet that broadly shares computer resources instead of using software or storage on a local PC. The term *cloud* is used as a metaphor for the Internet, based on the cloud drawing used in the past to represent the Internet in a computer network as an abstraction of the underlying infrastructure it represents. A technical definition of cloud computing is a computing capability that provides an

abstraction between the computing resource and its underlying technical architecture (e.g., servers, storage, networks), enabling convenient, on-demand network access to a shared pool of configurable computing resources that can be rapidly provisioned and released with minimal management effort or service provider interaction. It is a paradigm shift from the current use of PCs, whereby details are abstracted from the users who no longer have need of expertise in, or control over, the technology infrastructure "in the cloud" that supports them.

5. *Knowledge repository*: The knowledge repository can be viewed as a form of organizational memory, or as a set of stored artifacts that organizations acquire, retain, and bear on their present activities. Knowledge repositories store two types of knowledge. The first type is concrete information and knowledge in databases, documents, and artifacts. The second type is the representation of unstructured abstract information and knowledge of human actors. They serve two basic functions: representation (presenting the knowledge for a given context) and interpretation (providing the frames of reference and guidelines for knowledge application). Computer-based repositories incorporate a variety of knowledge forms ranging from data and text-based documents and models to digital images, video, and audio recordings.

6. *Knowledge portals*: A knowledge portal is an integrated set of knowledge management enabling tools and technologies. A portal can be described as a gateway or a one-step access to information and knowledge sources over the web. One of the key technologies used in knowledge portals is document management, which plays an important role in knowledge retention and knowledge organization. A primary function of any document management system is to allow the effective and efficient handling of large amounts of documents that originate from a variety of sources. Organizations produce and circulate large amounts of information every day, and document management systems are used to gather, store, and make this information searchable and available to users over the network. Document management systems use the imaging tools, optical character recognition tools, and database management systems.

7. *Knowledge organizing tools*: The features and characteristics of knowledge repositories vary from one organization to another, depending on the functionality of the repository and the types of applications deployed on the web server. Personalization of contents enables users to create their own personal workplace according to a set of preferences that enables them to view the contents they are interested in while having all irrelevant information automatically filtered out.

In order to organize the information and knowledge, the following tools can be used:

Ontology may be defined as "a formal, explicit specification of shared conceptualization" (Gruber, 1993). This implies that domain ontology provides us with a formalized vocabulary for describing a given domain.

Taxonomy, also called classification or categorization schemes, is considered to be a knowledge organization system that serves to group objects together based on a particular characteristic. It is relevant to use knowledge taxonomy for the organizing knowledge of the organization. Knowledge taxonomies generate hierarchical classification of terms that are structured to show relationships between terms. In the context of knowledge management tools, the term *ontology* is often used interchangeably with *taxonomy*, as this may be the operational conceptualization of a domain chosen by a user. To clarify the distinction, it is important to recognize that ontology is an overall conceptualization whereas taxonomy is a "scientifically based scheme of classification."

Folksonomy is a free-form indexing system developed through the collaboration of a community of users. It can be viewed as a user-generated and distributed system of categorization, emerging through bottom-up consensus. Its advantages are simplicity of use, flexibility, and rapid adaptability.

Attempts have been made to characterize folksonomy in social tagging systems as emergent externalization of knowledge structures contributed by multiple users. Models of collaborative tagging have been developed to characterize how knowledge structures could arise and be useful to other users, even when there is a lack of top-down mediation (which is believed to be an important feature because they do not need laborious explicit representations as in semantic webs).

2.5.2   Knowledge Capture Systems

Knowledge capture systems rely on knowledge management mechanisms and technologies that support externalization (conversion of tacit knowledge into explicit form) and internalization (conversion of explicit knowledge into tacit form). The articulation of stories is an example of a mechanism that enables externalization. Learning by observation and face-to-face meetings are examples of mechanisms that facilitate internalization. Technological support in knowledge capture systems for externalization and internalization includes the implementation of different intelligent technologies. Externalization can be realized by expert systems and case-based reasoning

(CBR) systems. Internalization can be facilitated by computer-based communication. By the help of such communication facilities, an individual can internalize knowledge from a message or its attachment sent by another expert. Artificial intelligence–based knowledge acquisition systems and computer-based simulation can also be used for internalization.

In the rest of this section, some useful technologies for knowledge capturing are described.

1. *Knowledge elicitation*: Knowledge can be either tacit or explicit. By definition the explicit knowledge is already captured in an understandable form. It is important to elicit tacit knowledge then capture it in a form that makes it easily manageable. The main vehicle for knowledge elicitation is face-to-face discussion between experts who possess the domain knowledge and knowledge workers who ask questions, observe the expert solving problems, and determine what knowledge is used. All these works are done manually. The automated capture of knowledge can be used from the database technique to build models of engineered system in CAD. It is powerful but limited in its applications.

2. *Search engines*: Search engines provide a standard interface for text searching and enable access to the unstructured information on the Internet. There are many commercial search engines allowing individual and organization to gather external third-party information. Search engine utilities also perform a similar function and provide access to large knowledge repositories on intranets and extranets.

3. *Intelligent agents*: Intelligent agents are software programs that act as personal or communication assistants to their users and carry out some sets of operations on their behalf with some degree of independence or autonomy. Intelligent agents that grew from expert systems and artificial intelligence research learn from data input during the course of their performance and modify their behavior accordingly. Task that agents can do include

    a. Retrieving documents

    b. Conducting a user-initiated search activity

    c. Maintain profile on behalf of their users

    d. Learning and deducing from user-specified profiles

    e. Assisting in the formalization of a query or target search

4. *Knowledge map*: The knowledge map is a feasible method of coordinating, simplifying, highlighting, and navigating through complex silos of knowledge artifacts. Knowledge maps point to knowledge, but they do not contain it. They are guides, not repositories. They usually point to people, documents, and repositories. The main purpose of knowledge maps is to direct people where to go when they

need certain expertise. In addition to the guiding function, knowledge maps may also identify strengths to exploit and knowledge gaps to fill.

5. *Knowledge-based system*: A knowledge-based system (KBS) is loosely defined as an interactive computer program that attempts to emulate the perception, reasoning, and learning process of experts in a given domain—a group of processes over which the expert makes decisions. Knowledge-based systems were originally devised as problem-solving techniques rather than frameworks for knowledge management systems. After many years, they were found to excel at representing human knowledge and became almost ideal tool for preserving and reusing the human knowledge required for problem-solving (Becerra-Fernandez, Gonzalez, and Sabherwal, 2004). In most cases, knowledge-based systems are considered adept at preserving knowledge. The knowledge-based system has two main modules: the knowledge base and the inference engine. The knowledge base includes the overall knowledge of the process as a collection of facts, methods, and heuristics, which are usually codified by means of heuristic rules. The inference engine is the software that controls the reasoning operation of the knowledge-based system, chaining optimally the knowledge contained in the knowledge base. The acquisition of the knowledge included in the knowledge base is the core and also the bottleneck of the knowledge-based system development. It involves eliciting, analyzing, and interpreting the knowledge that experts use to solve a particular problem (by "solve" we mean diagnosing the situation, detecting the cause, and proposing the suitable actuation).

2.6   Knowledge Discovery and Creation Technology and Systems

As pointed out in Section 2.4, the new explicit knowledge can be discovered and created through combination, integration, and systemization. Synthesis of new tacit knowledge can be realized through socialization with knowledgeable persons. These persons may have more experiences from the past or new ideas generated now. Knowledge can also be discovered by finding interesting patterns in observations, typically embodied in explicit data or text.

Mechanisms and technologies can support knowledge discovery by facilitating combination and socialization. Mechanisms that facilitate combination include collaborative problem solving, group decision making, and collaborative creation of documents. Mechanisms that facilitate socialization include apprenticeship, employee rotation across areas, conferences, brain storming retreats, cooperative projects across departments, and initiation process for new employees (Maier, 2007).

1. *Knowledge discovery in databases (KDD)*: KDD is the process of finding and interpreting patterns from data, and involves the application of algorithms to interpret the patterns generated by these algorithms. Data mining (DM) is another name of knowledge discovery in databases. Though the majority of the practitioners use KDD and DM interchangeably, in reality KDD is defined to involve the whole process of knowledge discovery including the application of DM techniques. In Chapter 5, the KDD techniques will be introduced in detail.

2. *Visualization tools*: Visualization tools are intended to assist people in analyzing complex data sets by mapping physical properties to the data. Visualization can map expertise, links between people across the organization and identify missing knowledge areas. Making organizational knowledge visible can support improvements and changes to the way knowledge is used, shared, and transferred. Some characteristics, such as light effects, color, direction, size, shadows, relative sizes and distance between objects, speed, curvature, and transparency are often used to help visualize data.

3. *Communication and collaboration techniques*: Various applications have been developed by using information and communication network to facilitate peer-to-peer communication. Examples include e-mail, bulletin board, chat room, white board, and audio and video conferencing. They also include various specialized groupware applications. The term refers to a particular type of application focused on collaborative processes among people. The peer-to-peer communication and computer-supported collaborative process can stimulate creativity and complex problem solving.

4. *Virtual reality*: Virtual reality technology enables people to be actively immersed in a simulated environment. It can have a dramatic impact on a number of areas including manufacturing, education and training, medical interventions, and military preparedness. Virtual reality offers a tool that enables people to learn more easily through experiential exercise rather than through memorizing rules.

5. *Mind games*: Mind games are a group of technologies focusing on fostering creativity and innovative problem solving. Most systems are designed to stimulate creative thinking based on the principles of associations, memory retrieval, and the use of analog and metaphor. In multiparticipant situations, it is also assumed that generation of creative ideas will be stimulated through participants' interaction where one idea leads to another and the process tends to build upon itself. A simulation game approach may also be helpful in solving complex problems. In a conventional management

game, one or more players have to make decisions in a simulated world. The game is played in a discrete number of rounds or periods. Once the players enter their decisions the results are computed and reported back to them. Normally the players can interfere with the simulated world at any time during a round or a period, and adjust their future strategies based on what they have learned from past experience and feedback.

6. *Creative process and techniques*: A variety of formal techniques have been developed to assist the production of novel ideas for decision making and innovation. Some of these techniques are limited to the idea generation aspect of the creative process, ignoring previous work and disseminating solutions. Most of the techniques are based on the notion that one may lose many creative ideas by evaluating them prematurely. Therefore, separation of the creation of ideas from their evaluation is an important aspect. Decision makers must not constrain themselves by rules when generating ideas. A popular expression that highlights this scenario is the need to "think outside the box." In general, it is believed that idea generation methods are important tools of encouragement for decision makers.

According to Handzic (2004), the idea-generation techniques can be classified into three basic categories (Marakas, 2003):

1. *Free association*: The most popular team-based free association technique is brainstorming. It is used to stimulate ideas without constraint, and the outcome is not permanent. Brainstorming also allows individuals or teams to capture all of their thoughts. It can be implemented electronically, manually, or verbally. Mind mapping is a method to record the free flow of ideas by drawing up a map that exchange the ideas of individuals. The ideas captured are without limit.

2. *Structured relationship*: The focus of the structured relationship is on the generation of new ideas through combinations of diverse ideas or concepts.

3. *Group techniques*: Group support systems (GSS) is a popular group technique for electronic brainstorming. Group brainstorming helps all group members to build upon their own and other group members' ideas. Ideas of each group member stimulate her own and others' thinking and produce new ideas for each individual. Group support systems contain group memory to store ideas generated by all individuals during the idea generation session. Other widely used group techniques include nominal group techniques (NGT) and the Delphi method, which involves a series of question and answer iterations until a convergence of responses is reached.

The role of information and communication technology in idea-generation is to facilitate the creation process, including generation, exploration, and communication of ideas. But the information that technology offered is only in explicit form.

2.7 Knowledge Sharing Technology and Systems

Knowledge sharing systems are designed to help users share their knowledge, both explicit and tacit. Most of the knowledge management systems in place at organizations are designed to share the explicit knowledge of individuals and organizations. There are two types of explicit knowledge sharing systems most widely introduced (Becerra-Fernandez, Gonzalez and Sabherwal, 2004). They are lesson learned system (LLS) and expertise-locator system (ELS). Systems that support tacit knowledge sharing are those typically utilized by communities of practice (CoPs), particularly those that meet virtually.

The standard communication medium on which knowledge management applications are based is the World Wide Web (WWW). It is a medium that facilitates the exchange of data, information, multimedia, and even applications among multiple distinct platforms. This characteristic of the web is referred to as platform independence. Because the web is pervasive and can be interfaced with different computer platforms through a common user interface, it is often the base on which knowledge sharing systems are created.

In the following text, some typical knowledge sharing systems are introduced.

2.7.1 Lesson Learned Systems

This kind of knowledge sharing systems have become commonplace in organizations and on the web. A lesson learned is knowledge or understanding gained by experience. The experience may be positive, as in a successful mission or test, and it may also be negative, as in a failure. The goal of lesson learned systems is to capture and provide lessons that benefit employees who encounter situations that closely resemble a previous experience in a similar situation.

The tasks of lesson learned systems are:

1. *Collect the lessons*: This task involves collecting the lessons that may be incorporated into the system. The collection process may be direct (from contributor) or indirect (contributor are interviewed by a third party for lessons and the third party submit the lesson), after-action or proactive, active or interactive.

2. *Verify the lessons*: The verification of lessons for correctness and redundancy are required. It is critically important, but it is time-

consuming and sometimes introduces a significant bottleneck in the inclusion of lessons into the system.

3. *Store the lessons*: This task relates to the presentation of the lessons in a computer-based system. It includes indexing of lessons, formatting, and incorporating into the repository.

4. *Disseminate the lessons*: Dissemination relates to how the information is shared to promote its reuse. There are six methods that can be used:

   a. passive dissemination,

   b. active dissemination,

   c. active casting,

   d. broadcasting,

   e. proactive dissemination, and

   f. reactive dissemination.

5. *Apply the lessons*: It relates to whether the user has the ability to decide how to reuse the lesson. There are three categories of reuse:

   a. Browsable: The system displays a list of lessons that match the search criteria.

   b. Executable: Users might have the option to execute the lesson's recommendation.

   c. Outcome reuse: When the system prompts users to enter the outcome of reusing a lesson, to assess whether the lesson can be replicated.

A similar knowledge sharing system is the best practices database. It differs from lesson learned system in that it captures only successful events, which may not be derived from experience.

2.7.2   Expertise-Locator Knowledge-Sharing Systems

Expertise-locator systems may serve different purposes across organizations. One purpose is to identify experts to help solve technical problems, or to perform gap analysis that point to intellectual capital inadequacies within the organization.

The intent of these systems is to catalog knowledge competencies, including information not typically captured by human resources systems, in a way that could later be queried across organizations.

1. *Access method of expertise locator system*: Most expertise locator systems are accessed via a company's intranet. Intranet is the popular

type of technology that handles all kinds of communication needs with ease. The inter-organizational systems are accessed via the web. Systems accessed via the web provide experts with increased level of visibility.

2. *Role of knowledge organization systems in the development of ELS*: In case of expertise locator systems, the knowledge taxonomy is used to describe organization's critical knowledge areas and used to index people's knowledge. Such kind of taxonomy must fulfill the following conditions:

   a. it should easily describe a knowledge area,

   b. it should provide minimal descriptive text,

   c. it should facilitate browsing, not complicate it, and

   d. it should have the appropriate level of granularity and abstraction.

Beside the taxonomy, there are also some tools like semantic networks, ontology, and authority files. Semantic networks serve to structure concepts and terms in networks or webs vs. the hierarchies typically used to present taxonomies. Ontology is relevant to knowledge management in that it is used to present complex relationships between objects as rules and axioms, which are not included in semantic networks. Authority files are lists of terms used to control the variant names in a particular field, and link preferred terms to non-preferred terms. Authority files are used to control the taxonomy vocabulary, particularly within an organization.

2.7.3 Community of Practices to Share Tacit Knowledge

Communities are groups of people who come together to share and learn from one another and who are held together by a common interest in a body of knowledge. Communities come together either face-to-face or virtually. They are driven by a desire and need to share problems, experiences, insights, templates, tools, and best practices. People come together because they are passionately interested in the topic and can receive direct value from participating in the community, because they are emotionally connected to the community. The community creates a cultural environment that promotes the socialization process and encourages the sharing of tacit knowledge. Many studies have demonstrated that any technological support for knowledge exchange requires users to believe they know and can trust each other. Therefore, the direct contact is necessary.

2.8   Knowledge Application Technology and Systems

Knowledge application systems support the process through which individuals utilize the knowledge possessed by other individuals without actually acquiring, or learning, that knowledge. To facilitate the knowledge management process of routines and directions, which do not necessarily need to comprehend the knowledge, some mechanisms and technologies based on the artificial intelligence can be used.

2.8.1   Types of Knowledge Application Systems

The common used knowledge application systems include the following:

1. *Help desk system*: The help desk provides a single point of contact for a user to get timely help with their technology or business needs. Some of the systems automatically retrieves from the case library historical cases similar to the one currently faced by the user.

2. *Fault diagnosis system*: The fault diagnosis system can detect, isolate, and analyze the fault and give suggestions for recovery. A great number of knowledge application systems over diverse domain have been developed for fault diagnosis since the first medical diagnosis system, MYCIN, appeared in the early 1970s. Creation of the case library will support this system.

3. *Expert system or advisor system*: Expert systems are designed to mimic human experts by applying reasoning methodologies of knowledge in a specific domain. The basic idea behind an expert system is as follows: First, expertise is transferred from an expert (or other source of expertise) to the computer. This knowledge is then organized and stored in the computer, and users can call on the computer for specific advice as needed. The computer can make inferences and arrive at a conclusion. Then, like a human expert, it offers advice or recommendations and explains.

4. *Decision support system*: A decision support system (DSS) is a computer-based information system that combines models and data in an attempt to solve semi-structured and some unstructured problems with extensive user involvement. A great variety of knowledge management technologies can be integrated into the system.

2.8.2   Technologies for Knowledge Application Systems

Most knowledge application systems are based on the techniques of a knowledge-based system, which had been based on the use of rules and models. Although the rules approach to knowledge representation has produced many examples of successful expert systems, many knowledge application systems are increasingly based on the implementation of case-based reasoning technology. Some technologies are listed and introduced below.

1. *Rule-based system*: The expert system discussed in the above is a typical example of this kind of system.

2. *Model-based reasoning system*: Model-based reasoning is an artificial technique used to reason with models to explain the case. Engineers, scientists, and highly skilled technicians often use the model to successfully handle problems and situations they have never seen before.

3. *Constraint-based reasoning system*: Many problems are defined by what cannot be done. The constraint system reflects what constraints restrict possible solutions. Constraint-based reasoning is a problem-solving technique that, when given a set of variables and constraints on these variables, can find a set of values that satisfy all the constraints. The name of this type of systems is *constraint-satisfaction system*.

4. *Case-based reasoning system*: An alternative to expressing knowledge as rules based on the heuristic knowledge of an expert is to express it explicitly in terms of historical problems that were once solved, and their solutions. Such an approach is called case-based reasoning (CBR). The most basic form of a case-based reasoning system consists of:

   a. a repository of historical cases called case library;

   b. a means to find and retrieve a similar case from the case library, and use its solution to solve current problem; and

   c. a means to add the newly solved problem and solution to the case library as a new case.

5. *Diagrammatic reasoning system*: Diagrammatic reasoning refers to the understanding of concepts and ideas through the use of diagrams and imagery, as opposed to linguistic or algebraic representations. The use of drawings for problem solving involves many of the same processes as using vision, which are scanning and perceiving. Drawings are used to present information about some problem in a form that can be visually extracted easily, instead of attempting to reproduce the real world.

3

Knowledge Management

Zhichang Zhu

University of Hull

CONTENTS

Knowledge is increasingly regarded as the only sustainable source for the continuous innovation and competitive advantage of individuals, organizations, and nations in the 21st century, where economies and human–ecology wellbeing are said to be knowledge based and knowledge management is seen as an indispensable means for survival, growth, and betterment. Adopting a pragmatic and holistic perspective, this chapter introduces readers to the theories and practices of knowledge-oriented management in organizations, which are composed of purposeful coping of three differentiated yet related areas: knowledge assets, knowing processes, and knower relations. It suggests that a systems approach promoting synergy among efficiency, creativity, and legitimacy will increase opportunities for organizations in the search for competitive advantage and sustainable prosperity. This chapter is a conscious attempt in bridging systems and knowledge sciences with an explicit focus on enhancing organizational management practices.

3.1 Toward Knowledge-Based Management

Knowledge management is not new. For thousands of years, parents in the countryside shared experiences with their children forecasting the weather;

owners of family businesses passed commercial wisdom to next generations; master craftsmen destroyed temples and rebuilt them so that construction skills would live on; and workers exchanged know-how on the job.
But it wasn't until the 1990s that corporate executives, university professors,
national leaders, and even the World Bank started talking about knowledge
management. What is new is that knowledge management has become a
consciously promoted and organized practice attached with strategic significance for organizations to pursue innovation, gain competitive advantage,
and improve performance.

Why does this change happen? Apart from the efforts of influential management thinkers such as Peter Drucker and Ikujiro Nonaka, several developments occurred that pushed knowledge management to the forefront of
business strategy and management. First, it is increasingly recognized that
the creation and maintenance of competitive advantage is not just about
scale, scope, and speed; it also demands continuous innovation. And innovation is not just about research and development (R&D)—enterprises compete
on innovations in, for example, technology, product, service, market, production process, organizational structure, corporate partnership, and business model. Hence, the management of technical and business knowledge
is regarded critical to success in the marketplace. Second, as globalization
rapidly spreads and deepens, firms are compelled to outsource activities for
optimizing their value chain globally, acquire and establish businesses off-
shore, and serve and create markets around the world. As a result, sources
of new knowledge are becoming geographically dispersed, which demands
effective coordination. Finally, the development of high-speed and low-
cost computer, communication, and other information technologies makes
it possible for organizations to collect, store, analyze, and transmit widely
distributed information at affordable prices. This enables firms to transform
business processes and opens up knowledge transfer needs and opportunities. In this changed, and still changing, competition landscape, knowledge
is thus increasingly taken as the strategic source of continuous innovation,
and knowledge management is the critical means for sustainable competitive advantage (Teece, 2008).

But what is knowledge, and is it manageable? These are highly philosophical questions, yet they have direct relevance and implications for business
practices. If we do not know what knowledge is, then what are we to manage? And if knowledge turns up unmanageable, what is the point of "knowledge management"?

The bad news is that, despite continuous debates on these fundamental
questions since Aristotle and Confucius's time, which have consumed our
best minds, there appear no consensual answers. Indeed, knowledge is such
a complicated and controversial subject that we humble human beings currently know very little about how it is created and whether it can be managed
at all. This is also true for knowledge-related constructs, e.g., (organizational)
capabilities or competence. We all take that these things are valuable for

improving organization performance (however performance is defined), but they are difficult to pin down—what is, and is not, knowledge or capability, and how do we manage it (Foss, 2009)?

Of course, there is no lack of conceptual schemes for classifying data, information, and knowledge—some scholars even extend their schemes to include wisdom on the top of knowledge, as if the more complicated the scheme the better. There is also a big jump from data-mining to "knowledge-discovery" models and techniques, which are loved by software companies and knowledge engineers. But when put into practice, it quickly becomes clear on the shop floor and in the laboratory that scholarly schemes often confuse more than they intend to clarify; for example, if I share with you via the Internet a report of a successful project, am I sharing data, information, knowledge, or wisdom? And knowledge mining is usually a more attractive label for data-mining models looking for new buyers.

Despite all these confusions and dilemmas, however, given the increasing competition, deepened globalization, and rapid technology change we cannot leave knowledge, which is fundamental to the life and death of organizations, to chance. Organizations face a dilemma: We do not know what knowledge is, but we must manage it, and now.

The good news is that there is a way forward—a pragmatic approach, this chapter would posit. We may not have a universal, once-and-forever definition of knowledge, but we can act upon a working understanding of it for practical purpose—an understanding not capturing the truth but a useful one that allows us to accomplish what we want in specific situations. We may not be able to predict or control knowledge in the way we manage land, machines, and the finance balance sheet, but we can nevertheless design organization structures, processes, and policies to influence the behavior of managers and workers so that they would likely create, share, and use knowledge willingly. We may not have one-size-fits-all knowledge management models or programs, but we can at least supply some lessons and insights based by which reflective managers can learn their own ways to benefit from the knowledge embedded in the assets, processes, and relationships within and beyond their organizations. It is for these reasons we appreciate Nonaka and his colleagues' (Nonaka, Toyama, and Hirata, 2008) recent promotion of knowledge-based management.

In this chapter, a pragmatic approach is taken to knowledge-based management that gears managerial efforts and organization resources to the following:

- Get the knowledge vision right
- Focus on organizational manageable
- Make it work in particular contexts

In the following pages, we explore the three components of knowledge-based management in some detail. These are not meant to be final conclusions but hypotheses from which to work.

3.2   Getting the Knowledge Vision Right

A knowledge vision denotes our understanding of what is relevant, important, useful, and operable in knowledge management for improving organizational performance. It shapes the purposes, problems, methods, and solutions of knowledge-related programs and is therefore chiefly determining the effectiveness, success, or failure of organizations' knowledge-promoting efforts. Organizations all have knowledge visions, articulated or otherwise, in the way that we, as individuals or as groups, all have views of the world. We may not recognize this, but our knowledge visions (and worldviews) underlie our knowledge-related initiatives and investments all the time. It is hence the job of leaders, policy makers, and managers to surface, challenge, share, and transform the knowledge visions of organizations when initiating and investing in knowledge management efforts. As any single person's vision is limited, managers need to do this job together with relevant stakeholders, for example, other managers, workers, customers, business partners, and the local community. This is for two reasons: first, since knowledge programs produce impacts on the well-being of stakeholders, from a moral perspective they should have their say; and second, it is the stakeholders' individual as well as collective efforts that make knowledge programs work (or fail). It is therefore important that stakeholders share the knowledge vision, and this will happen only when they participate in the ongoing processes of challenging, maintaining, and transforming those visions.

It is useful to examine an organization's knowledge vision via two conceptual devices: a locus scope and an action framework (Figure 3.1). Let us begin with a knowledge locus scope.

3.2.1   Content Scope

A knowledge locus scope concerns a pragmatic question: "What do we need to know for solving problems at hand?" Let's take a marketing executive's position. For one thing, the company needs to deliver products and services to the marketplace in technically efficient ways, for which her staff act on operational research and engineering knowledge.

For another, market researchers must understand customer preferences that are not always "rational," for which they seek humanity and cultural knowledge. Further, as public relations and social changes shape consumers' conceptions of the company's activities, which ultimately determines

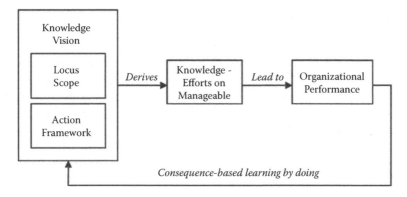

FIGURE 3.1
From knowledge vision to organizational performance.

the company's competitiveness and survival, the marketing executive turns to knowledge in business ethics, sociology, and political economics. Useful knowledge hence comes to us in many forms from various disciplines, such as from natural sciences and engineering for investigating the material world, from psychocognitive studies for understanding our mental world, and from sociopolitical inquiries for coordinating our social world. This applies to public policy making, too: Sound decisions upon whether, and how, to build the Three Gorge Dam on China's Yangzi River, to reform Japan's postal system, to transform the UK pension provision, and to tackle World Trade Organization (WTO) disputes among nations all demand proper data gathering, rigorous model building, informed public debate, and legitimate political action, for which wide ranges of heterogeneous sources and different forms of knowledge are indispensable. Our scope about knowledge locus matters.

Our survey reveals that research and practice on knowledge scope commonly cover three analytically differentiated yet empirically interconnected dimensions: knowledge assets, knowing processes, and knower relations (Zhu, 2008):

1. Knowledge asset: Along this dimension, knowledge is seen as embodied in, for example, tools, equipments, and electronic document systems. In managing knowledge assets, the emphasis is on capturing, stocking, and transmitting what people know by the means of scientific logic, engineering principles, programmable methodologies, and information-communication technologies. While we should be cautious against the idea that knowledge management is all about building huge web-based protocols, complicated "knowledge bases" or agent-based simulation, we must take effort to enable knowledge sharing with available and affordable technologies. Technology is a bad master but can be a good servant to knowledge-based management. One small story demonstrates

this (BBC, 2008).* A British doctor in Democratic Republic of Congo conducted a forequarter amputation on a local boy—the boy was badly infected due to losing most of his arm in the crossfire between government and rebel forces. The doctor, who had never performed such an operation before, proceeded by receiving instructions from an experienced doctor in London via texting messages back and forth during the operation. The operation was successful, and the boy survived. Without knowledge sharing via the mobile phone between "knowledge workers," he would certainly have died. Other successful examples include British Petroleum's worldwide Virtual Teamwork Stations and Hewlett-Packard's Lotus Notes customer service database.

2. Knowing process: This dimension focuses attention on how people know and how their knowing can be enhanced for achieving organizational success. Nonaka's knowledge creation process model is perhaps the most influential in this regard (Nonaka and Takeuchi, 1995). The model conceptualizes knowledge creation as a series of epistemological conversions between tacit and explicit knowledge: socialization, externalization, combination, and internalization (SECI), which work along an ontological spiral that moves up and down among individual, group, organization, and interorganization levels. Significantly, the SECI conversion model brings culture in and stresses the context-specific, practical, social, and spiritual aspects of knowledge creation. It is about both ideas and ideals, skills and emotion. Knowledge is created while organizations solve problems, but people don't just solve problems—they create and define them according to their vision, values, and the searching of common goodness. The model posits that knowing processes as such cannot be managed by the predict-and-control convention or scientific principles. Rather, the spiral conversions are facilitated by *ba*, care, love, and teamwork, and the means to achieve these are proper organizational structure, culture, incentive, metaphors, and distributed leadership (for further theoretical elaboration and practical business cases such as Seven-Eleven Japan, Eisai, YKK, and Muji see, e.g., Nonaka et al., 2008).

3. Knower relations: This dimension is concerned with diverse interests, power configurations among knowledge workers (indeed, all employees and stakeholders), and the consequences in the market economy. If knowledge has value and is scarce, why should we give it out freely? Particularly, if you are to be laid off tomorrow—even in Japan this is becoming more often—are you to contribute more to the organization knowledge base today? Organizations, industries, and

---

* BBC. Surgeon saves boy's life by text. December 3, 2008. http://news.bbc.co.uk/go/pr/fr/-/1/hi/health/7761994.stm.

countries may have built knowledge superhighways, but would any-one drive on them without knowing what has to be paid for it? After all, why are there patents, copyrights, legal contracts, and intellectual property lawsuits? Who will benefit from knowledge management: stockholders, executives, or workers? Let's face it: We have created more knowledge, and perhaps have managed it more efficiently, but the gap is getting wider between the rich and the poor, the haves and have-nots, and our home Earth is in an unprecedented alarming state. Don't forget: just recently, it was the new knowledge created in the banking sector, some of them programmed into automatic stock-trading knowledge system, that brought the world economy into a deep recession (Grant and Mackenzie, 2010). No wonder surveys and case studies repeatedly confirm that the knower issue is regarded by managers as the most decisive and challenging in knowledge man-agement (Johnson, Lorenz, and Lundvall, 2002; Ruggles, 1998).

To put it metaphorically, managing knowledge assets emphasizes the "high-tech," enhancing knowing processes amounts to "high-touch," and caring knower relations is about handling "high fences." We call this a holistic scope. It underscores the complementary and reciprocal interconnectedness among knowledge assets, knowing processes, and knower relations in the creation and maintenance of superior organizational advantage (Figure 3.2).

The problem is, according to research findings, too often the knowledge scopes underlying many knowledge efforts are too narrow to accommodate the complexity and complementarities among knowledge assets, knowing processes, and knower relations. Knowledge-promoting programs are usu-ally designed to manage merely assets, processes, or knowers, respectively. Knowledge management means different things to different people and lacks a bigger picture wherein various knowledge-related efforts can inter-act with each other, as if changes in one will not introduce or demand any

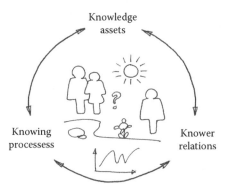

FIGURE 3.2
A holistic knowledge scope.

change to or from the other (Assudani, 2005; Powell and Swart, 2005; Roberts, 2004). Organizations claim they value their human resources while at the same time lay off workers and middle managers ruthlessly in the names of efficiency and productivity, for instance (Mintzberg, 2007; Reich, 2010). While diversity, including that in knowledge management, has great value, it is not an unqualified virtue. When coupled with a reductionist mind-set, it induces dissipation not synergy, and it destroys rather than improves organizational performance. Hence, we need to consider high-tech, high-touch, and high-fence efforts as parts of the knowledge management whole to ensure that the whole is bigger, not smaller, than the sum of its parts. It is imperative to remind ourselves that the performance of a system obviously depends on the performance of its parts, but an important, if not the most important, aspect of a part's performance is how it interacts with other parts to affect the performance of the whole. "Therefore, effective systems management must focus on the interactions of its parts rather than on their actions taken separately" (Ackoff, 1994, p. 180).

It is in this regard that a holistic scope has much to offer. The process of surfacing, questioning, and transforming our knowledge scopes nurtures an inclusive approach since it encourages managers and workers to talk to each other, to construct a bigger picture—never complete but always changing—that connects focal knowledge initiatives to organization-wide purpose, strategy, and practice.

3.2.2 Action Framework

Action framework can be seen as a bridge that translates an organization's knowledge scope into actionable initiatives. The premise is that, even with a holistic scope, effective activities do not occur spontaneously but need to be promoted, supported, and coordinated. This is so because, as indicated in Section 3.1, knowledge-oriented efforts, if effective, cannot be left to chance but must demand constant managerial attention. If locus scopes explore "What is important?," then action frameworks figure out "What to do?" in knowledge-based management.

While every organization has its knowledge scope, holistic or narrow-minded, articulated or otherwise, this is not so in action frameworks. Action frameworks are usually intentionally created or adopted by managers for the purpose of mobilizing organizational commitment, resources, and energy toward collective actions, in contrast with ad hoc, let-what-happens-happen behavior. Action frameworks can be formal or informal, driven from an intuitive gut feeling or deliberate plan. Given that knowledge efforts should ideally permeate an organization's every level and division, owned by every worker, manager, and wider stakeholder, a well-thought-out and articulated action framework has the advantage of being communicated and shared effectively. Of course, well-thought-out action frameworks need not necessarily be in a formal, structured format. It all depends on organizational contexts. Sometimes, metaphors, analogues, and storytelling will do a good job; at other times, clear statements and formal deliberations are needed.

We take Leonard-Barton's (1992) four-action-area framework as an exemplar. The rationale of our choice is not because four is the magic number. Managers may choose three, five, or other four action areas as their own "what to do" according to their organization's circumstances. We introduce Leonard-Barton's action framework (with our interpretation and reconstruction though) as the starting point because it is well informed by holistic thinking—Leonard-Barton calls it "an organic system view" and is highly compatible with our embracing knowledge-knowing-knower scope.

The Leonard-Barton (1992) framework focuses managerial attention on four knowledge-oriented action areas along two dimensions. Along the present–future dimension are situated problem solving and continuous experimentation, and along the internal–external dimension are integrating internal knowledge and incorporating external knowledge activities. Let us have a brief look at them one by one (Figure 3.3).

The situated problem solving action area manifests a pragmatic orientation: solving real problems in here-and-now life experience is the starting point and destination of human actions. Knowledge creation is not about finding time-and-context-free truths but about improving our capacity to act (i.e., to define and solve problems) in specific situations. Knowledge-based management should therefore benefit organizations by solving pressing problems in

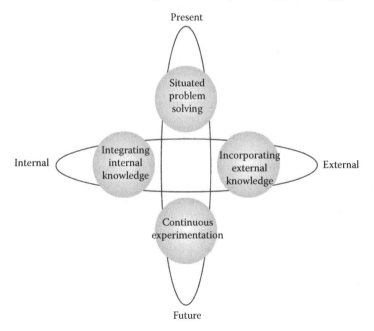

FIGURE 3.3
A holistic action framework. (Based on Leonard-Barton, D., *Sloan Management Review*, 34, 1, 1992.)

current operations. Knowledge management is therefore not to burn money but for creating and capturing value. Without this down-to-earth, pragmatic orientation and convincing cost-effective evidence, no knowledge program or initiative can be viable.

The "continuous experimentation" area releases knowledge efforts from short-term traps and enables organizations to pursue long-term competitive advantage. Innovation, the engine of organizational excellence, is by definition doing something unconventional, something new; there is always risk. No risk, no gain. When experimentation stops, innovation dies. Promoting continuous experimentation demands, and nurtures, a positive attitude toward risk, which allows organizations to learn from mistakes as well as successes. Without continuous experimentations guided by a future orientation that balances short-term performance and long-term success, there can be no sustainable competitive advantage.

The integrating internal knowledge area encourages sharing and cooperation across functions and projects in an organization. Because of increasing division of intellectual labor, knowledge in modern organizations is widely dispersed. Successful companies combine distributed, heterogeneous internal technology, and business knowledge and design them into innovative products and services that lead the market. Knowledge creation happens when people interact with each other. It is everyone's job and ideally takes place along the whole internal value chain or market chain in all organizational processes, across organizational divisions, in a well-coordinated manner.

The incorporating external knowledge area promotes an open business model for knowledge-based management. In the face of rapid technology change and fast-moving marketplace, as products and services become increasingly complex and interconnected organizations' ability to tap a larger variety of knowledge sources through a rich portfolio of business partnerships is crucial. Organization members' competence to absorb and use knowledge from outside is as important as creating knowledge internally. For this, successful companies even cooperate with competitors and seek knowledge complementarities on many fronts: production design, marketing, and distribution. The "not invented here" mentality is a recipe for killing knowledge creation, innovation, and competitive advantage.

This broadly structured framework draws managers' attention to the core activities that are vital to knowledge-based management. Ideally, the four action areas should be taken as a corporate ecosystem (Leonard-Barton, 1992). Focusing on one single area while ignoring or downplaying others will not work. Focusing on immediate problem solving alone would compromise the company's ability to imagine and realize a valued future, whereas frenetic experimentations isolated from solving company's pressing problems are unlikely sustainable, and combining distributed knowledge both inside and outside organizations for continuous innovation has increasingly become common sense. A knowledge-creating company, or a learning organization, cannot be constructed piecemeal. Knowledge-based management success depends on the intense interconnectedness and complementarities among efforts in all the action areas. It is the constant managerial attention on, and skillful coordination of, all the activities, not just doing one or two activities well, which enables companies to achieve excellence. This is why successful companies do not mind opening themselves up to visitors, even to rivals—the whole knowledge-based management ecosystem is difficult to imitate. Visitors may take away this or that component, but that will not work for them. This happened in total quality management, and it is also true for knowledge management. The upshot of all this is that, for effective knowledge-based management, managers need to construct a holistic action framework for promoting and coordinating their knowledge-promoting efforts. For this purpose the action framework we present here is a good starting point.

A content scope and an action framework together constitute an organization's knowledge vision about what is important and what to do in knowledge-based management. Based on research findings on business practice, this chapter suggests that a holistic knowledge scope that embraces knowledge assets, knowing processes, and knower relations and an organic action framework that nurtures a corporate action ecosystem are useful for originations to build their sustainable competitive advantage on continuous innovation fueled by knowledge creation.

3.3   Focusing on Organizational Manageable

While knowledge visions shape our understanding of what is important and what to do, in this section we move on to explore how to do it. Since, as we explained earlier, we still lack agreement on what knowledge is and know very little about the exact process through which knowledge is created, it is fruitful to try to manage the unmanageable, that is, to manage knowledge or to intervene in the knowledge creation process directly. We have no choice but to focus on managing the manageable.

What are the manageable for promoting knowledge then? It is useful to consider and structure the manageable based on the knowledge vision introduced in Section 3.2. In each of the four action areas, managers, together with stakeholders, can propose concrete activities. Such activities, intended to promote knowledge creation and innovation, may be suggested based on an organization's own experiences, brainstorming exercises, benchmarking other organizations, surveying business media and relevant literatures, and consulting business leaders and management thinkers.

Furthermore, it is important to consider, in each of the action areas, what values underlie and promote the intended activities. People do things based on, and motivated by, the meaning they attach to them. They commit only to

FIGURE 3.4
Triad of organizational manageable. (Based on Leonard-Barton, D., *Sloan Management Review*, 34, 1, 1992.)

those activities they valued. Values are not things to hold on to, pass around, manufacture, or control. Values need to be continuously renegotiated, re-created, and shared. All these, for facilitating effective knowledge management, need to be directed and supported by managerial systems such as organizational structure, promotion policies, compensation mechanisms, motivation incentives, and resource allocation. Together, knowledge-oriented activities, underlying values and supportive managerial systems, constitute a triad of organizational manageable (Figure 3.4).

Combining a holistic knowledge vision and the triad of organizational manageable into a managerial platform, like a balanced scorecard (Kaplan and Norton, 2005), would enable stakeholders to, in a systemic and informed manner, propose, discuss, justify, promote, evaluate, and coordinate knowledge management efforts, which should not be a one-shot exercise of box-filling but needs to be continuously tested, reflected upon, and reworked (Table 3.1).

TABLE 3.1

Combining knowledge vision with manageable triad into knowledge-promoting managerial platform

Manageable triad Knowledge vision	Knowledge- oriented activities	Underlying values	Supportive managerial systems
Situated problem-solving			
Continuous experimentation			
Integrating internal knowledge			
Incorporating external knowledge			

TABLE 3.2

Useful Knowledge Management Practices

Useful Practices	Activities	Values	Systems
Situated problem solving	Establishing problem ownership, job design for on-the-spot problem solving or R&D	Respect for each person, egalitarianism, "it is good to make do"	Performance rewards, dissolving R&D boundaries, internal market chain
Continuous experimentation	Challenging conventional wisdom, asking why five times, *kaizen* programs, "even if it isn't broken, fix it," eliminating 20% of current product offering every year	Disciplined risk taking, tolerance to failure, "it is a shame not to innovate"	"Fast mistakes" award, "devil's advocate," dedicated time and resources for personal pet projects, hiring enthusiastic employees, clear path for career advancement
Integrating internal knowledge	Open offices, enabling people to see each other frequently, encouraging accidental meetings, away days, knowledge conferences, knowledge surveys, information technology infrastructures connecting people together	Knowledge sharing, "it is wise to learn from others"	Job rotation, cross-functional teams, mentoring schemes, formal apprenticeship, corporate education, on-the-job training
Incorporating external knowledge	Cooperative joint projects, frequent visit to business partners and customers, attending industry-wide conferences and workshops, benchmarking competitors	Openness, "not reinvented here"	Formal partnerships, boundary elements, corporate intelligence and travel budgets

Table 3.2 illustrates some reported practices in the business media and research literature that are said to be useful for effective knowledge management. This should be taken as merely a very brief indication showing possible directions for managers to start their learning-by-doing processes; it is not meant to be exhaustive or conclusive, let alone must-do principles.

3.4 Making It Work in Particular Contexts

Knowledge scopes, action platforms, and manageable triads, even holistic ones, are not ready, one-best-recipes for organization success. Organizations differ. In the real world, no two companies are the same. Homogenous firms as production units in neoclassical economics are merely fictitious creatures for theoretical convenience. Just look at General Motors and Ford, Sony, and Fujitsu: Even in the same industry and the same country, they vary greatly. Firms have different histories and organizational DNAs, pursue different strategies, possess different knowledge assets, develop different knowing routines, and consist of people with enormously diverse expectations, preferences, and relationships. Hence, there can be no one-size-fits-all knowledge programs or must-do lists that guarantee good results for all. To complicate matters, environments continuously change and organizations constantly regenerate themselves, for better or worse. Successful formulas even for the same organization quickly become obsolete. Given all this, how can organizations proceed for effective knowledge-based management, and what are knowledge vision and manageable triad good for?

We posit that knowledge-based management is, broadly understood, an inquiry process and that all human inquiries can be seen as underlying a generic logic. In *How We Think* (Dewey, 1910), the American pragmatist thinker, education reformer, and social activist John Dewey presented the generic logic as encompassing five related activities:

1. Making sense of felt difficulties or problematic situations
2. Defining issues and problems
3. Hypothesizing (dis-)solutions
4. Developing and justifying the bearings of the suggested solutions
5. Acting up hypothesized solutions, learning from consequences— and the inquiry continues

We call this a generic logic because it appears generally applicable to human inquires, or problem solving, in all organizations in various sectors, industries, and situations. In our life experience, we all proceed along this logic, just more or less consciously, reflectively, and skillfully. And knowledge visions and manageable triads can be used to inform our judgment, imagination, justification, and action along the several logical steps in knowledge management:

In Step 1, for example, managers and workers may find their organization leaking knowledge to competitors, leaving behind market demands, facing increased customer complains, and witnessing high employee turnover. It is useful to make sense of these concerns through the conceptual lenses of a holistic *knowledge scope*: Are the difficulties likely associated with the organization's mishandling of knowledge assets, ignoring knowing process, or deteriorating knower relations?

In Step 2, stakeholders use an *action framework* to define issues and problems, mapping them to or deriving them from the four differentiated yet interrelated action areas: solving immediate problems, experimenting for long term success, sharing knowledge throughout the organization, and incorporating knowledge from beyond organizational boundaries.

In Step 3, participants, informed by *manageable triads*, propose and deliberate on possible programs, projects, and policies for solving or dissolving the defined issues and problems. As indicated earlier, all these steps can be supported by a wide range of skills, tools, and techniques, such as reflecting on an organization's past experiences, benchmarking good performers, using metaphors and analogues, surveying literature and media, and brainstorming.

In Step 4, the focus is that implementation matters, for example, resources and constraints, costs and effects, timing and structure, likely impacts on stakeholders, contingent alternatives. This step puts all the talking into walking: processes and effects are constantly observed; experiences are reflected on; successes and failures are learned from; and programs and policies are changed if necessary for doing better.

During this knowledge-based management process, which is broadly undergirded by the generic inquiry logic as depicted by Dewey (1910), it is imperative to note the following: First, it should be a pragmatic, flexible, spiral process. Participants may spend longer time and more energy in some steps while shorter and less in others; the boundaries between steps are subjective and naturally fuzzy; participants may move contingently between steps of the process or toward the next round of the experimental spiral; the steps may be taken as fairly formal or very informal—we are engaging in process full of uncertainty, not following fixed procedures regardless; we act upon the logic for achieving valued outcomes not for performing the steps per se. Whatever works—just do it. The correct ways we act upon the generic inquiry logic all depend on circumstances, on situated particulars. One best way of doing things, including doing knowledge management, is illusive forever. Our judgment, justification, skill, and creativity make the differences. Always look at the real process, happenings, and outcomes; embrace surprises and exploit accidents; learn, improve, and change accordingly, quickly.

Second, creativity and innovation are the keys for effective knowledge-based management. Having a me-too strategy or seeking universal, context-free programs are dead ends. With imitating best practice alone, the best we can achieve is catching up. Following others, however excellent they are, will never make you a winner. It is hopeless and self-contradictory trying to copy best practice for knowledge creation and innovation. You cannot promote innovation without your own innovative means; knowledge creation can be enhanced only through creative managerial undertakings. Benchmarking is not about becoming the same but about differentiation, doing different things, and doing things differently. This is why in promoting knowledge management, in presenting John Dewey's (1910) generic inquiry logic, we insist on avoiding the temptation to supply readers with ready, prescriptive, detailed must-do lists. Rather, we post a fundamental challenge to managers: While there is great value in understanding and appreciating others' successes, in the end you must learn your own way for workable and beneficial knowledge-based management—workable and beneficial for *your* organization. There is no better way than experimental learning by doing.

Finally, knowledge-based management, if effective, is a collective enterprise with collective purposes, collective intelligence, and collective efforts. We already, throughout this chapter, presented the moral, instrumental, and operational cases for interactive participation. Knowledge, in view of action in the world, is our capacity to define and solve problems in specific situations. Technologies and machines may help, but it is fundamentally human centered, a human thing. Knowledge is not merely about minds, let alone just brains; it is also about hearts. As Nonaka puts it, "Knowledge needs value judgment to be knowledge" (Nonaka et al., 2008, p. 8). Accordingly, to know is to enlarge our capacity to solve situated problems, to take timely actions, to make valued differences, to make our ideas real. We do not need knowledge with which humans harm each other or exploit Mother Earth efficiently; we want knowledge to envision and realize common goodness, properly, effectively, joyfully. We do not need casino financial innovations; we want a netbook in every child's hands, a successful football World Cup in Africa, and a greener environment for all. Knowledge management should be a positive, inspiring, enabling, consequential project of enlarging humankind's potential, as persons as well as communities, in companies, industries, regions, and society. Knowledge-based management is a communal undertaking. It cannot be achieved by a chief knowledge officer (CKO) or the chief executive officer (CEO) alone. If it can, we do not need all the managers and workers; organizations can be conveniently downsized to the CKO and CEO. This may sound like common sense; the point is to make it work, to translate it into real knowledge management process, in specific organizations, in particular contexts.

3.5   Conclusion

This chapter introduces readers to knowledge-based management. Although we focus on business organization and corporate strategy for presentation convenience, we consider the ideas in the chapter equally applicable in other sectors (e.g., government bodies, public agencies, research institutes, and universities). Leaders, managers, and employees in all these various sectors do need to think very hard about how to coordinate their knowledge assets, learning routines and motivation issues, how to promote activities in immediate problem-solving, experimentation for the future, and integrating knowledge both inside and outside their organizations.

The premise of the chapter is that we do not know for certain what knowledge is or how to manage it directly but that we cannot leave the creation and use of knowledge to chance given the increasing competition, deepened globalization, and fast technology change. To create knowledge continuously and capture value from it for collective purpose, what we can do is approach knowledge management pragmatically; that is, focus on handling organizational manageable with underlying values and supporting managerial systems instead of modeling knowledge (we still have difficulty in agreeing on what knowledge is) or modeling the processes of creating it (we, humbly, know so little about such processes). In a pragmatic spirit, we introduce a knowledge scope that promotes managing knowledge-embodied assets, enhancing employees' knowing process, and caring for knower relations. To translate knowledge scope into action, managers can organize their knowledge-promoting effort based on the fabric of four interrelated broad action areas: immediate problem solving, experimenting for the future, integrating internal knowledge, and incorporating useful knowledge from outside an organization. In each of the action areas, each organization, a manufacture company or a university laboratory, should decide which detailed activities are useful and workable in their particular contexts. A five-step generic inquiry logic revealed by John Dewey (2010) is useful for facilitating the whole process of proposing, justifying, and acting upon these organization-specific activities. Knowledge-based management is about getting the vision right, focusing on manageable, and making it work in specific contexts. It is matters of intelligent making-do, fallible inquiry, and consequence-based learning, purposefully, experimentally, creatively, and collectively.

"*Tao* is made on the walking of it," the Taoist Zhuang Zi famously said. We hope you make your own path in managing knowledge creatively, effectively, and beneficially.

4

Knowledge Discovery

Tu Bao Ho

Japan Advanced Institute of Science and Technology

CONTENTS

Knowledge discovery and data mining (KDD) emerged as a rapidly growing interdisciplinary field that merges together databases, statistics, machine learning, and related areas to discover and extract valuable knowledge in large volumes of data. With the rapid computerization in the past two decades, almost all organizations have collected huge amounts of data in their databases. These organizations need to understand their data or to discover useful knowledge as patterns or models from their data. Meeting this increasing need in the digitalized society, KDD has been becoming an attractive science and technology in both theory and practice. This chapter will provide basic concepts and methods of KDD as well as its typical applications. It starts by providing an overview of data, information, and knowledge and then definitions of knowledge discovery and data mining. It is followed by the steps in the KDD process. The main part of the chapter deals with the essential ideas of typical KDD methods and the challenges and trends of KDD after its 15 years of development. Finally, text mining—a typical branch of KDD—and its application will be briefly introduced.

4.1   Introduction

Knowledge science is the science of creating and using knowledge by humans and machines. As addressed in the introduction chapter, our view is knowledge creation, and its use can be fundamentally established by integrating management science, information science, and systems science. In these ingredients of knowledge science, knowledge management essentially is about how humans create and use knowledge; information science essentially is about how machines can support humans in creating and using knowledge; and systems science essentially is about how humans and machines can create and use knowledge in their diversity.

There are different ways by which knowledge is created; one that has been long used by humans is obtaining knowledge through observing and analyzing the phenomena happening around them. In the era of computers and the Internet, phenomena are observed, measured, accumulated as data stored in databases, and computation programs help in the analysis of these data. The knowledge discovery addressed in this chapter is an information science ingredient of knowledge science, which is essentially the finding or discovering knowledge in data. It is an interdisciplinary field, having roots in database management, statistics, and machine learning and has emerged in the new field of knowledge discovery and data mining in the last two decades (Han and Kamber, 2006; Hand, Mannila, and Smyth, 2001).

Knowledge discovery has developed quickly and has attracted the interest of people not only in academy but also in industry. Its fast development can be attributed to an increasing number of international events; it emerged from several workshops in the early 1990s, the first international conference on knowledge discovery in databases was held in August 1995 in Montreal. Originally known as ACM SIGKDD, KDD has quickly become a top conference topic in information science held annually in North America. Since 1997, there have been annual Pacific Asia conferences on knowledge discovery and data mining (PAKDD) and European conferences on principles and practice of knowledge discovery in databases (PKDD), which in 2001 merged with the European Conference on Machine Learning (ECML) as ECML/PKDD. Soon after that, several other well-recognized conferences on knowledge discovery surfaced such as IEEE ICDM and SIAM DM. The name of the KDD field has also changed with time. In the early years it was commonly called *knowledge discovery in databases,* but in the last decade the names *knowledge discovery and data mining* or simply *data mining* have become popular and often used (the latter is not to be confused with one of the five steps in the KDD process called "data mining").

To have a simplified idea about what *finding knowledge in data* means, let's recall the notions of data, information, and knowledge. Though there are no single definitions of these notions on which scholars agree, the common view in information science is the following:

Data are essentially uninterpreted signals that we can daily observe, measure, and collect.

Information is processed data equipped with meaning.

Knowledge is integrated information or generalized data, including facts and their relations.

If we count the number of cars on a road by hours, by days of the week, or by months, we have data; if we compute the average of number of cars each hour, each day, each week, or each year on the road, we have information from the data; if we can state that road is appropriate or not for such amount of cars, we have knowledge. The key question in knowledge discovery is how to go from data to knowledge.

This chapter aims to presents the key notions, methods, and development in knowledge discovery and its contribution to knowledge science. Section 4.2 addresses different aspects of knowledge discovery with emphasis on the discovery process. Section 4.3 briefly introduces key techniques of data mining in a simple but essential way for readers with background in other fields to understand. Section 4.4 introduces text and web data mining—two subfields of knowledge discovery that have received much attention and play a significant role in knowledge discovery. Section 4.5 focuses on mining scientific data and provides some examples about the data mining in medicine, biology, and materials science. Section 4.6 concludes the chapter and addresses some features of the future development of knowledge discovery.

4.2 Knowledge Discovery and Data Mining

4.2.1 Definition and Examples

Knowledge discovery and data mining can be defined the automatic extraction of nonobvious, hidden knowledge in the form of patterns or models from large volumes of data (Fayyad, Haussler, and Stolorz, 1996). Throughout this chapter we will illustrate diverse notions concerning knowledge discovery using real-world data. Following are examples from the meningitis database collected

TABLE 4.1

Attributes in the meningitis database

Categories	Type of attributes	Number of attributes
Present History	Numerical and Categorical	7
Physical Examination	Numerical and Categorical	8
Laboratory Examination	Numerical	11
Diagnosis	Categorical	2
Therapy	Categorical	2
Clinical Course	Categorical	4
Final Status	Categorical	2
Risk Factor	Categorical	2
Total		38

at the Medical Research Institute at the Tokyo Medical and Dental University from 1979 to 1993. This database contains data of patients who suffered from meningitis and who were admitted to the departments of emergency and neurology in several hospitals. Table 4.1 presents attributes used in this database. The following are data records of two patients in this database with mixed numerical and categorical data as well as missing values (denoted by "?"):

```
10, M, ABSCESS, BACTERIA, 0, 10, 10, 0, 0, 0, SUBACUTE, 37,
    2, 1, 0, 15, -, -6000, 2, 0, abnormal, abnormal, -, 2852,
    2148, 712, 97, 49, F, -, multiple,?, 2137, negative, n,
    n, n
12, M, BACTERIA, VIRUS, 0, 5, 5, 0, 0, 0, ACUTE, 38.5, 2, 1,
    0, 15, -, -, 10700, 4, 0, normal, abnormal, +, 1080, 680,
    400, 71, 59, F, -, ABPC+CZX,?, 70, negative, n, n, n
```

A pattern discovered from this database by our method Learning Unbalanced Positive Class (LUPC) (Ho and Nguyen, 2003) implemented in the system D2MS (Ho, Nguyen, Shimodaira, and Kimura, 2003) in the form of if–then rules is given as follows; the quality of the pattern is measured by its coverage and accuracy:

```
 IF  Poly-nuclear cell count in CFS ≤ 220
and  Risk factor = n
and  Loss of consciousness = positive
and  When nausea starts > 15
THEN  Prediction = Virus [coverage = 13, accuracy = 87.5%]
```

This rule among others discovered from the meningitis patient data can be viewed as a pattern. In knowledge discovery, a *pattern* is a local structure of a data set, a low-level summary of a relationship, perhaps that holds only for a few records or for only a few variables. In contrast, a *model* is a global description of a structure that summarizes the systematic components underlying the data or that describes how the data may have arisen (Hand et al., 2001). Examples of discovered models, as we will see later, can be a regression hyperplane, a hierarchy of clusters, a decision tree, a neural network, or a set of rules.

Extracting knowledge from data is also the target of machine learning and explanatory data analysis in statistics. *Machine learning* (ML) has the goal of building computer systems that can adapt and learn from their experience. A computer program is said to learn from experience E with respect to some class of tasks T and performance measure P, if its performance at tasks in T, as measure by P, improves with experience (Bishop, 2006; Mitchell, 1997). Machine learning problems can be formulated as given a set of n pairs $(x_1, y_1), (x_2, y_2), \ldots, (x_n, y_n)$, where x_i is description of, for example, an object or a phenomenon, and y_i is some property of x_i (if y_i is not available, the learning problem is called unsupervised), to find a function $f(x)$ that $f(x_i) = y_i$. The function f here is in fact also patterns or models learned from the data.

The era of computerization and the Internet has also led to significant changes in statistics. Classical multivariate statistics methods can analyze only flat data sets with moderate size and thus yield poor results for huge and complex data. Also, computational costs of storing and processing data have crashed over the past decade (Izenman, 2008). The *exploratory data analysis* (EDA) initialized by Tukey in 1977—in contrast to confirmatory data analysis that emphases on statistical hypothesis testing—aims at using data to generate hypotheses to test. Those hypotheses in fact are also patterns and models as mentioned previously. Knowledge discovery and data mining, machine learning, and explanatory data analysis share not only an inductive nature but also the same broad goal of finding novel and useful knowledge.

The main differences among them are their emphases on different aspects of data handling. While machine learning focuses more on theoretical aspects of computation mostly of symbolic data and explanatory data analysis focuses more on extension of statistical methods mostly of numerical data, knowledge discovery and data mining focuses more on real-world data that are large and complex.

It is worth noting that these three fields have been developed closely with each other, and they alternatively establish computational methodology for knowledge discovery in a broad meaning.

4.2.2 Knowledge Discovery Process

The process of knowledge discovery can be viewed as inherently consisting of five steps (Ho, Kawasaki, and Granat, 2007). The main tasks in each step of the KDD process are shown in Figure 4.1.

The first step is to understand the application domain and formulate the problem. This step is clearly a prerequisite for extracting useful knowledge and for choosing appropriate machine learning and data mining methods in the third step according to the application target and the nature of the data.

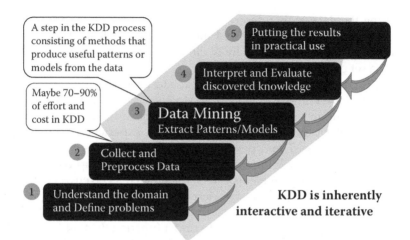

A step in the KDD process consisting of methods that produce useful patterns or models from the data

Maybe 70–90% of effort and cost in KDD

5 Putting the results in practical use

4 Interpret and Evaluate discovered knowledge

3 Data Mining
Extract Patterns/Models

2 Collect and Preprocess Data

1 Understand the domain and Define problems

KDD is inherently interactive and iterative

FIGURE 4.1
The KDD process.

The second step is to collect and preprocess the data, including the selection of the data sources, the removal of noise or outliers, the treatment of missing data, the transformation (discretization if necessary), and the reduction of data. This step usually takes the most time in the KDD process, as much as 70–90% as seen in many knowledge discovery applications (Pyle, 1999).

The third step is data mining to extract patterns or models hidden in the data. The major classes of data mining methods for the two main tasks of prediction and description are classification and regression; segmentation (clustering); dependency modeling, such as graphical models or density estimation; summarization, such as finding the relations between fields; association; visualization; and change and deviation detection and modeling in data and knowledge.

The fourth step is to interpret (postprocess) the knowledge discovered by methods having inductive nature. Experiments show that discovered patterns or models from data are not always of interest or direct use, and the KDD process is necessarily iterative with the judgment of discovered knowledge. Generally, each data mining task has its own criteria and measures for evaluation. For example, the standard way to evaluate a classification method is to split the data into two sets: the training data is used to discover new knowledge and the testing data is used to evaluate the discovered knowledge. One can repeat this process a number of times with different splits and then average the results to estimate the method's performance.

The final step is to put discovered knowledge into practical use. Sometimes, one can use discovered knowledge without embedding it in a computer system. In other cases, the user may expect that the discovered knowledge can be put on computers and exploited by various programs. Putting the results to practical use is certainly the ultimate goal of knowledge discovery.

4.2.3 Model Selection in Knowledge Discovery

The *model selection* in knowledge discovery, as well as in machine learning or explanatory data analysis, is given a data set and some analysis task, to identify the most appropriate methods and its parameter settings to best do the analysis task. As shown in Figure 4.2, at the data-mining step we need to select the data-mining tasks and then the data-mining methods before carrying out knowledge extraction. However, to have appropriate results we need to go through the step of testing and refining discovered knowledge carefully, and those steps may have to be done in iteration. Also, it is important to have basic background about the variety of data to be mined and the nature of different data-mining methods that can be used appropriately in different circumstances. Thus, model selection in knowledge discovery can be viewed in two dimensions: (1) the type of data to be mined and (2) the mining tasks and methods.

Several aspects related to the data should be considered in knowledge discovery. First, one needs to distinguish whether the data are supervised or unsupervised. If data objects in the database are known to be instances of predefined categories or object groups, they are called *supervised* or *labeled* where the attribute characterizing the categories or groups is *class* attribute. If data objects do not have such property, they are *unsupervised* or *unlabeled*. For supervised data, the main analysis task is prediction, whereas for unsupervised data the main analysis task is description (described in Section 4.3).

Various kinds of data are stored in different data schemes. The typical schemes include flat data tables, relational databases, object-oriented databases, object-relational databases, and transactional databases. Data are collected from various fields having different natures, such as spatial databases,

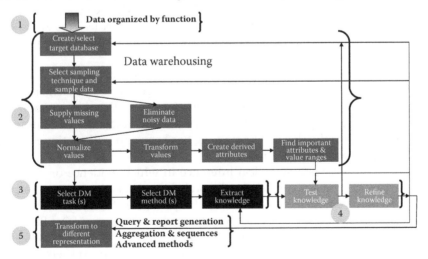

FIGURE 4.2
Main tasks in each step of the KDD process. (From Gehrke, J., Tutorial on Knowledge Discovery and Data Mining, PAKDD, 2000.)

temporal databases and time-series databases, text databases and multimedia databases, heterogeneous databases and legacy databases, and World Wide Web data (Han and Kamber, 2006).

4.3 Data-Mining Techniques

4.3.1 Data-Mining Methods

Data-mining tasks and methods basically can be divided into two groups: (1) classification/prediction and (2) description. Classification/prediction is the process of finding a set of models or patterns or functions that describe and distinguish data classes or concepts, for the purpose of being able to use the model to predict the class of objects whose class label is unknown. *Classification* usually stands for the case when class attribute has discrete values, whereas *prediction* usually stands for the case when class attribute has continuous values. Description is the process of characterizing the general properties of the data in a database.

Typical methods of classification and prediction include (Bishop, 2006; Han and Kamber, 2006; Hand et al., 2001; Mitchell, 1997; Hastie, Tibshinari, and Friedman, 2008; Izenman, 2008) the following:

Decision-tree induction aims to find classification models in the tree structure where each internal node denotes a test on an attribute; its outcomes are branches from the node and leaf nodes represent classes or class distributions. Typical decision-tree methods are C4.5 and CART. Recent research on decision trees includes converting large trees into sets of rules, tree visualization, data access (to very large databases) and random forests, an ensemble method with decision trees.

Neural networks are information-processing devices that consist of a large number of simple nonlinear processing modules, connected by elements that have information storage and programming functions. Extracting or making sense of numeric weights associated with the interconnections of neurons to come up with a higher level of knowledge has been and will continue to be a challenging problem in data mining.

Bayesian inference is a statistical inference in which evidence or observations are used to update or to infer the probability that a hypothesis may be true. The name Bayesian comes from the frequent use of the Bayes's theorem in the inference process. The most widely used methods are Naïve Bayesian classification, assuming that attributes are all independent, and Bayesian belief networks, assuming that dependencies exist among subsets of attributes. Representing dependencies among random variables by a graph in which each random variable is a node and the edges between the nodes represent conditional dependencies is the essence of the graphical models that play an increasingly important role in machine learning and data mining (Jordan, 1998).

Rule induction produces a set of if–then rules from a database. Unlike decision-tree methods that employ the "divide-and-conquer" strategy, rule induction methods mostly employ the "separate-and-conquer" strategy. Some popular methods include CN2, IREP, RIPPER, and LUPC (Ho and Nguyen, 2003; Pham and Ho, 2007).

Hidden Markov models (HMM), a widely used finite-state-machine method, are statistical models in which the system being modeled is assumed to be a Markov process with unknown parameters, and the challenge is to determine the hidden parameters from the observations. Recent finite-state-machine methods, including maximum entropy Markov models (MEMM) and conditional random fields (CRFs), have shown their high performance in various structured prediction problems.

The following are some typical description methods (Bishop, 2006; Han and Kamber, 2006; Hand et al., 2001; Mitchell, 1997):

Association rule mining, which aims to discover elements that co-occur frequently within a data set consisting of multiple independent selections of elements (e.g., purchasing transactions) and to discover rules, such as implication or correlation, which relate co-occurring elements. Questions such as "If a customer purchases product A, how likely is she to purchase product B?" and "What products will a customer buy if she buys products C and D?" are answered by association mining algorithms. Typical association mining algorithms are Apriori and FP-tree (Han and Kamber, 2001). A typical example of association mining from IBM is that by analyzing supermarket data unexpected rules can be detected such as "Many young men often buy diapers and beer together." Recently, Han et al. (2007) provided an excellent overview of the current status and future directions for research on association rule mining.

Clustering seeks to identify a finite set of categories or clusters to describe the data. The categories may be mutually exclusive and exhaustive or may consist of richer representations such as hierarchical or overlapping categories. Examples of clustering in knowledge discovery include discovering homogeneous subpopulations for consumers in marketing databases or the identification of subcategories of spectra from infrared measurements. Data-mining research focuses on efficient and effective clustering methods for large and complex databases (e.g., scalability, complex shapes and types of data, high dimensional clustering, mixed numerical and categorical data).

Summarization involves methods for finding a compact description for a subset of data. A simple example would be tabulating the mean and standard deviations for all fields. More sophisticated methods involve the derivation of summary rules, multivariate visualization techniques, and the discovery of functional relationships between variables. Summarization techniques are often applied to interactive exploratory data analysis and automated report generation.

It is worth noting that most data-mining methods are originally developed in a general form; for example, the decision-tree algorithm C4.5 originally designed for flat data tables. They should be changed and adapted appropriately when being applied to different types of data, such as text or graph data.

Visualization has proven its effectiveness in exploratory data analysis and has great potential in data mining. Various methods and systems have been developed for visualizing large data sets and discovered knowledge (e.g., large decision trees, huge numbers of associations) as well as visualizing the knowledge discovery process (Figure 4.3). They facilitate and support the active role of the user in all knowledge discovery steps, from preprocessing to interpretation and evaluation (Fayyad, Grinstein, and Wierse, 2001; Ho, Nguyen, Kawasaki, Le, Nguyen, Yokoi, and Takabayashi, 2003; Nguyen, Ho, and Kawasaki, 2006).

Finding *scalable* algorithms is a typical requirement in data mining to deal with huge data sets. An algorithm is said to be scalable if, given an amount of main memory, its runtime increases linearly with the number of input instances. Massively parallel processing is another strategy for dealing with huge data sets when the algorithm in nature cannot be so nearly linear to be scalable (Freitas, Simon, and Lavington, 1998).

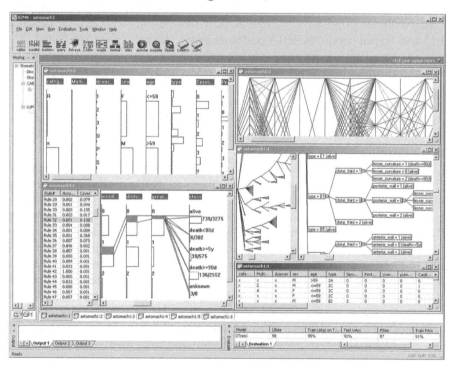

FIGURE 4.3

Different views of decision tree in system D2MS. (From Ho, T.B., Nguyen, T.D., Shimodaira, H., Kimura, M., *Applied Intelligence*, 19, 125–141, 2003.)

Various new techniques have been developed to attack these problems. In the last decade, kernel methods (Schölkopf and Smola, 2001), graphical models (Jordan, 1998), and semisupervised learning (SSL; Chapelle, Schölkopf, and Zien, 2006) have emerged among the most exciting research directions in machine learning and data mining.

Kernel methods in general, and *support vector machines* (SVMs) in particular, are currently of great interest to theoretical researchers and applied scientists. SVMs have been very successful in building highly nonlinear classifiers and also in dealing with situations in which there are many more variables than observations. They offer versatile tools to process, analyze, and compare many types of data and offer state-of-the-art performance in many cases. The big problem with simple models of linear learning machines (e.g., perceptrons, developed in 1956) is that of insufficient capacity. The first wave of neural networks (since the mid-1980s) overcame the problem by gluing together many thresholded linear units (multilayer neural networks). That solved the problem of capacity, but there were training problems in terms of speed and multiple local minima. The kernel methods approach in the last decade can be viewed as the second wave of linear learning machines. The key idea of kernel methods is instead of finding a nonlinear classifier for data objects $x_1, x_2, \ldots, x_n$, which are only not linearly separable in an original description space X, one transforms them into data objects $\varphi(x_1), \varphi(x_2), \ldots, \varphi(x_n)$ in a feature space Φ by some mapping $\varphi: \to \Phi$ and find a linear classifier for these objects $\varphi(x_i)$, $i = 1, 2, , n$ in Φ. The inverse mapping φ^{-1} allows establishing the corresponding nonlinear classifier in X. It is very interesting to note that the learning process is not carried out in the feature space Φ but on a kernel matrix obtained by a kernel function $k: X \times X \to \Re$ that maps each pair of data objects in $X \times X$ into a real number and has the property that $k(x_i, x_j) = \langle \varphi(x_i), \varphi(x_j) \rangle$, where $\langle \varphi(x_i), \varphi(x_j) \rangle$ is the inner product of $\varphi(x_i)$ and $\varphi(x_j)$ (Schölkopf and Smola, 2001; Schölkopf, Tsuda, and Vert, 2004).

Graphical models are a marriage between graph theory and probability theory (Jordan, 1998). They clarify the relationship between neural networks and related network-based models such as HMMs, Markov random fields (MRFs), Kalman filters, and CRFs. Typical advantages of graphical models are that inference and learning are treated together; supervised and unsupervised learning are merged seamlessly; missing data are handled nicely; there is a focus on conditional independence; and there is a high interpretability of the results.

Semi-supervised learning is halfway between supervised and unsupervised learning. In addition to unlabeled data, the algorithm is provided with some supervised information—but not necessary for all examples. Often, this information will be the targets associated with some of the examples (Chapelle et al., 2006, p. 2). As a relatively new area of machine learning, it is a new learning paradigm of great interest in both theory and practice.

A good introduction to the ten most frequently used algorithms in knowledge discovery and data mining can be found in Wu et al. (2008).

4.3.2   Challenges in Data Mining

The main feature of knowledge discovery is that it deals with large and complexly structured data. This is reflected in the 10 most challenging problems of this field, identified by many active and influential researchers at the IEEE International Conference on Data Mining 2005 (ICDM'05) and published one year later (Yang and Wu, 2006):

1. Developing a unifying theory of data mining
2. Scaling up for high-dimensional data/high-speed streams
3. Mining sequence data and time-series data
4. Mining complex knowledge from complex data
5. Data mining in a network setting
6. Distributed data mining and mining multiagent data
7. Data mining for biological and environmental problems
8. Data-mining process-related problems
9. Security, privacy, and data integrity
10. Dealing with nonstatic, unbalanced, and cost-sensitive data

4.4   Text and Web Mining

Text is the largest source of human knowledge accumulated over time, and the web is a new but fast growing source of human knowledge. Text mining and web mining thus have a particular role in knowledge discovery and knowledge science.

4.4.1   Text Mining

The enormous amount of texts stored in computers and computer networks are thought to contain the largest amount of human explicit knowledge that can be exploited only by advanced computation methods.

Like data mining, *text mining* can be viewed as the nontrivial extraction of implicit, previously unknown, and potentially useful information from (a large amount of) textual data. In other words, we can define text mining as data mining (applied to textual data) plus language engineering. It means that text mining can be viewed as applications of machine learning and statistics methods to texts with the goal of finding useful but hidden patterns, trends, and associations (Hotho and Numberger, 2005; Franke, Nakhaeizadeh, and Renz, 2003; Weiss, Indurkhya, Zhang, and Damerau, 2006).

One typical example of text mining is the work carried out by Swanson and Smalheiser (1997). When investigating causes of migraine headaches, they extracted various pieces of evidence from titles of articles in the bio-medical literature, for example:

- Stress is associated with migraines.
- Stress can lead to loss of magnesium.
- Calcium channel blockers prevent some migraines.
- Magnesium is a natural calcium channel blocker.
- Spreading cortical depression (SCD) is implicated in some migraines.
- High levels of magnesium inhibit SCD.
- Migraine patients have high platelet aggregability.
- Magnesium can suppress platelet aggregability.

These clues suggest that magnesium deficiency may play a role in some kinds of migraine headaches. It meant that a new, potentially plausible medi-cal hypothesis that did not exist in the literature was induced by combining culled text fragments with human medical expertise.

Text mining closely relates to several other areas, typically natural lan-guage processing (NLP), information retrieval, information extraction, web mining, and regular data mining:

Natural language processing aims to automate language understanding (Jurafsky and Martin, 2008; Manning and Schutze, 2001). In fact, we have a long way to go before we reach machine understanding of the human lan-guage, but various subgoals of text analysis have been partially achieved. The process of going from text to its meaning can be divided into four typical steps and levels: lexical/morphological analysis, syntax analysis, semantic analysis, and discourse analysis. The main tasks in lexical and morphologi-cal analysis include word segmentation (to separate words in a sentence in languages such as Chinese or Japanese), part-of-speech (POS) tagging for each term (to determine the part of speech tag, e.g., noun, verb, adjective), and chunking (to group adjacent words in a sentence, such as to chunk "the current account deficit" as a noun phrase). The main tasks in syntactic analy-sis include grammatical relation finding, named entities recognition, word sense disambiguation, and parsing. Semantic analysis aims at understanding the meaning of word and sentences, whereas discourse analysis addresses languages in practice.

Information retrieval (IR) is the finding from a source of textual documents a set of (ranked) documents that contain answers to questions. To achieve this goal statistical measures and methods are used for the automatic processing of text data and comparison with the given question. Current systems that retrieve documents based on keywords (i.e., systems that perform document retrieval like most search engines, typically Google) are frequently also called information retrieval systems. Information retrieval has changed considerably in the last few years with the expansion of the World Wide Web and the advent of modern and inexpensive graphical user interfaces and mass storage devices (Baeza-Yates and Ribeiro-Neto, 1999; Manning, Raghavan, and Schutze, 2008).

Information extraction (IE) aims at automatically extracting from text documents the information relevant to the well-defined query of the user. Information extraction is a specific type of information retrieval, and especially information extraction from the web is getting more attention from both researchers and users. The web contains huge sources of documents that are daily creating and updating, and no one can keep up with such fast changes. IE on the web is expected to help people to find something needed on a pages but not just the page itself.

4.4.1.1 Text Encoding

Most corpora contain the plain text files, and to mine them it is necessary to encode and then store them in their appropriate formats. Text encoding usually has three main parts: (1) text preprocessing, (2) text representation in a vector space model, and (3) linguistic preprocessing.

Text preprocessing usually starts by *filtering* methods to remove the stop words, which are words that bear little or no content information, like articles, conjunctions, and prepositions, and to remove words that occur either extremely often or very seldom (according to Zipf's law). It is followed by *lemmatization* methods to map verb forms to their infinite tense and nouns to the singular form and then *stemming* methods try to build the basic forms of words, such as strip the plural "s" from nouns, the "ing" from verbs, and other affixes. After the stemming process, every word is represented by its stem. Another important step is the *index term selection* to choose a number of key words to represent the document. A simple technique to do it is selection of key words based on their entropy.

After selecting a set of key words to represent each document in the text collection, the next hurdle is how to represent the documents. Currently, the most popular method to representing huge document collections is the *vector space model*, which is efficient for many tasks in text mining as well as in information retrieval. The vector space model represents documents as vectors in m-dimensional space; that is, each document d is described by a feature vector $w(d) = (x(d, t_1), \ldots, x(d, t_m))$, where m is the number of total distinct words (or terms) obtained from the collection, and $x(d, t_i)$ is the word t_i if it occurs in d and empty vice versa. Usually, each word t_i selected from the set of total words $\{t_1, t_2, \ldots, t_m\}$ to represent the document d is associated with a weight $w(d, t_i)$ that reflects the importance of t_i in d in the relation to the whole collection. The computation process for these weights is called term weighting and the most popular way is to use the measure of $tf - idf$ defined by

$$tf - idf(x(d, t_i)) = tf(x(d, t_i)) \times idf(x(d, t_i))$$

where term frequency $tf(x(d, t_i))$ is number of occurrences of term t_i in d, the inverse document frequency $idf(x(d, t_i)) = \log(N/df(t_i))$, where $df(t_i)$ is the number of documents in the collection of totally N documents that contain the term t_i (document frequency). The $tf - idf(x(d, t_i))$ of a document d is also often normalized by its length to ensure that all documents have equal chances of being retrieved independent of their lengths. Based on a weighting scheme a document d is defined by a vector of term weights $w(d) = (w(d, t_1), \ldots, w(d, t_m))$. In fact, only words having weights greater than zero or some threshold will be selected, and thus the representation is also called a bag of words.

Usually, most text-mining methods exploit the text collection where each document is represented in a vector space model as a bag of words. Some tasks, however, may require further *linguistic processing*, often at the level of shallow parsing with the text analysis for POS tagging, chunking, grammatical relation finding, and with named entities recognition, word sense disambiguation, and syntax parsing.

4.4.1.2 Typical Problems and Applications

Typical text-mining tasks include text categorization, text clustering, document summarization, trend detection, sentiment and opinion analysis, information extraction, question answering, entity relation modeling (i.e., learning relations between named entities), and text visualization. We will briefly introduce some of them.

Text categorization is the problem of assigning one or more labels from a predefined set to a document based on its content. It is the task of classification in machine learning. The main difference is that, whereas data classification generally is a single-label classification problem where each example in the training data is associated with a single label, text categorization typically is a multilabel classification problem where each example in the training data is associated with a set of labels. One example of text categorization is patent classification. Each year there are about 1.6 million new patents registered around the world, and about 400,000 in Japan. When a new patent, described as a semistructured text, is applied for, a task is to check if a similar patent already exists and how to assign it to categories of patents in the system. Note that the International Patent Classification (IPC) is the most widely used patent classification system where patents are assigned to categories corresponding to their main application domain and topic. Additionally, the F-term classification system developed by the Japan Patent Office (JPO) classifies patents from multiple viewpoints (e.g., materials used, operations, problems addressed, and solutions proposed). The problem is determining, given a new applied patent, which subset of F-terms (as labels) will be assigned to the new patent. Common methods for text categorization are also classification methods in machine learning with adaptation to the textual documents represented as mentioned already. Those include Naïve Bayesian classification, decision trees, support vector machines, and neural networks.

Text clustering is a specific problem of data clustering with the task of organizing unsupervised documents. The quantity of electronic documents on the web is quickly increasing, making it difficult for users to browse or to identify relevant information; thus, automatically grouping the documents into a list of meaningful categories would be of great help. Most clustering methods can be applied to do clustering texts with some specific issues for consideration. For example, the main target of grouping similar documents into the same clusters requires understanding to some extent the content or meaning of the documents or how to label the clustered created by identifying their theme. One way to do it is to display the contents of the clusters by showing typical terms and typical titles, to ask the user to choose subsets of the clusters, and to recluster the documents within resulting new groups have different themes.

Text summarization is relatively new technology to deal with the phenomenon of information overload where the purpose is the creation of a shortened version of a text by a computer program. Thus, a text is entered into the computer, and a summarized text is returned, which is a nonredundant extract from the original text. Broadly, there are two main approaches to text summarization: extraction and abstraction. The extraction approach aims to copy the most important information of the text to the summary, while abstraction aims to generate a short text that paraphrases the gist of the document. A typical process of text summarization may consist of three steps: sentence extraction (find a set of important sentences that covers the gist meaning of the text document); sentence reduction (convert a long sentence to a short one without losing the meaning); and sentence combination (combine sentences to make a text).

Trend detection aims to discovering the most significant changes in the data from previously measured values. Trend detection from textual data aims at exploiting available text to predict what may happen in the future, for example, the future trend of a product type in next 6 months in the market. An attractive problem in this area is *emerging trend detection* defined as detecting topic areas that are growing in interest and utility over time (Le, Ho, and Nakamori, 2005).

Going from text to its meaning is the ultimate goal of language processing, and it is a long road to reach the final goal. It is well known that the keystones on this road are *latent semantic analysis* (Deerwester, Dumais, Furnas, Landauer, and Harshman, 1990), its extension to probabilistic latent semantic analysis (Hofmann, 1990), and *topic modeling* (Blei, Ng, and Jordan, 2003). Latent semantic analysis creates from vector space of documents a new space of latent variables (usually with much small number of dimensions), each of them a linear combination of original variables, and then it represents and analyzes the documents in the new latent semantic space. Topic modeling has recently attracted much research attention as it is promising in capturing the semantics of text. The key idea is to represent each document as a mixture of latent topics, where a topic is a probability distribution over words. The topics will be learned from large corpora and used for various applications; for example, someday search engines could perform a search by given topics and not just by key words as they do currently.

Text mining has various possible applications; for example, analyzing plain text sources such as the Internet news for security purposes, helping a scientist detect findings in literature related to a topic under investigation, and analyzing the customer relationship management in marketing applications.

4.4.2 Web Mining

Data mining turns data into knowledge, and *web mining* can be viewed as applying data-mining techniques to extract and uncover knowledge from web documents and services (Chakrabarti, 2001; Kosala and Blockeel, 2000; Liu, 2007). Web mining closely relates to several other areas, typically information retrieval, information extraction, text mining, and regular data mining. In the aspect of information searching, web mining can be viewed as a part of the (web) information retrieval process. In the aspect of learning to extract patterns/rules, web mining can be viewed as a part of the (web) information extraction process.

The web is a huge source of information for knowledge discovery. According to the Netcraft web server survey, the number of websites worldwide in June 2010 is about 240 million (http://news.netcraft.com/archives/category/web-server-survey). Web mining has several features that make it different from other branches of data mining. Websites are widely distributed with highly heterogeneous content (e.g., text, image, voice) and are organized in semi-structured networks as well as linked by hypertext and hypermedia.

Web-mining technology can be divided into three types: web content mining, web structure mining, and web usage mining.

Web content mining is discovery of information from web contents (e.g., textual, image, audio, video, hyperlinks). The web content data consist of unstructured data such as free texts, semistructured data such as HTML documents, and a more structured data such as data in the tables or databases generated by HTML pages. There are two points of view on web content mining: The information retrieval view is mainly to assist or to improve the information finding or filtering the information, and the database view mainly tries to model the data on the web and to integrate them so that more sophisticated queries other than key words could be performed.

Web structure mining is discovery of the model underlying the link structures of the web. The model is based on the topology of the hyperlinks with or without the description of the links. The discovered model can be used to categorize web pages and is useful to generate information such as the similarity and relationship between different websites. Web structure mining could be used to discover authority sites for the subject (authorities are pages to which many pages link) and overview sites for the subjects that point to many authorities (hub sites). Some algorithms have been proposed to model the web topology; typically two recursive ones are PageRank and HITS.

PageRank is a link analysis algorithm used by the Google Internet search engine, developed by its two founders Larry Page and Sergey Brin (Brin and Page, 1998). PageRank assigns a number to each website, called a PageRank number, computed by the PageRank algorithm (Brin and Page, 1998), to measure the relative importance of the webpage on the web. The PageRank of a webpage is defined recursively and depends on the number and PageRank metric of all pages that link to it (incoming links). A webpage that is linked to by many pages with a high PageRank receives a high rank itself. If there are no links to a web page there is no support for that page.

HITS (Hyperlink-Induced Topic Search) is another link analysis algorithm that rates webpages and was developed by Jon Kleinberg (1999). HITS determines two values for a page: its authority, which estimates the value of the content of the page; and its hub value, which estimates the value of its links to other pages.

Web usage mining is the discovery of information from web users' sessions and behavior (secondary data derived from the interactions of the users while interacting with the web). Some users might be looking at only textual data, whereas some others might be interested in multimedia data. Typical data sources used in web usage mining include automatically generated data stored in server as access logs, referrer logs, agent logs, and client-side cookies, or user profiles as well as metadata such as page attributes, content attributes, and usage data. Various data-mining techniques can be applied to analyze those data, especially association and sequence analysis, clustering and classification. Examples of the patterns discovered can be "Clients who often access /products/software/webminer.html tend to be from educational institutions" or "75% of clients who download software from /products/software/demos/ visit between 7:00 and 11:00 pm on weekends."

4.5   Scientific Data Mining

Due to the rapid progress of network and data acquisition technologies in the last decade, a huge amount of data has been accumulated and archived in many scientific areas, such as astronomy, medicine, biology, chemistry, and physics. To find useful information in these data sets, scientists and engineers are turning to data analysis techniques. There has been a fundamental shift from more conventional techniques to computer-aided scientific discovery in various sciences, especially by using machine learning and data-mining methods to exploit these huge and precious scientific databases (Augen, 2005; Gilbert, 1991; Lacroix and Critchlow, 2003; Langley and Simon 1995; Ramakrishnan and Grama, 2001).

It is worth noting that scientific data are essentially complexly structured data (e.g., temporal data, biological sequences, materials structures, text, dynamic graphical networks; Figure 4.4) that create a number of difficulties when being analyzed (e.g., structured output interdependency, imbalanced, heterogeneous, and large scale).

This section introduces a new branch of computer science: mining scientific data (Fayyad et al., 1996; Kamath, 2009). On one hand, the progress in machine learning and data mining has opened various opportunities for scientific discovery through scientific data. On the other hand, the complexity of scientific data raises many challenging problems for data-mining researchers. Importantly, the collaboration between domain experts and computer scientists is always a key factor in successful scientific data mining.

The role of scientific data mining is well recognized. "Given the success of data mining in commercial areas, it didn't take much time for the scientists and engineers to discover the usefulness of data mining techniques in scientific disciplines. For example, analysis of massive simulation data sets generated by computational simulations of physical and engineering systems is difficult and time consuming using traditional approaches. Indeed, much of the output of computational simulations is simply stored away on disks and is never analysed at all. Availability of suitable data mining techniques can allow engineers and scientists to analyze such data and gain fundamental insights into the underlying mechanisms of the physical processes involved" (Grossman, Kamath, Kumar, and Namburu, 2001).

On the surface, it may appear that data from one scientific field, such as genomics, are very different from another field, such as physics. Despite this diversity, there is much that is common in the mining of scientific data. For example, the techniques used to identify objects in images are very similar, regardless of whether the images came from a remote sensing application, a physics experiment, an astronomy observation, or a medical study. Further, with data mining being applied to new types of data, such as mesh data from scientific simulations, there is the opportunity to apply and extend data mining to new scientific domains.

FIGURE 4.4
Scientific data typically have a complex structure.

4.5.1   Mining Medical Data

Evidence-based medicine (EBM) applies the scientific method to medical practice and aims for the ideal that healthcare professionals should make *conscientious, explicit, and judicious use of current best evidence* in their everyday practice. Generally, there are three distinct, but interdependent, areas of EBM. The first is to treat individual patients with acute or chronic pathologies by treatments supported in the most scientifically valid medical literature. The second area is the systematic review of medical literature to evaluate the best studies on specific topics. The third is the medical *movement*, in which advocates work to popularize the methods of EMB and the usefulness of its practice in public forums, patient communities, educational institutions, and the continuing education of practicing professionals (Cios, 2000).

Following is an example of the practical implementation of EMB. Viral hepatitis is a disease in which tissue of the liver is inflamed by the infection of hepatitis viruses. As the severity of viral hepatitis increases, so does the potential risk of liver cirrhosis and hepatocellular carcinoma (HCC)—which is the most common type of liver cancer and the fifth most common cancer. While the exact cause of HCC is still unknown, studies on viral hepatitis, especially on hepatitis types B and C, have become essential in medicine. The hepatitis relational temporal database, collected from 1982 to 2001 at Chiba University Hospital in Japan, was recently released to challenge the data-mining research community. This database contains results of 983 laboratory tests on 771 patients. It is a large, uncleansed, temporal relational database consisting of six tables, the biggest of which has 1.6 million records. The doctors posed a number of problems on hepatitis that could be investigated by KDD techniques. We have worked on mining the hepatitis data to solve several problems raised by physicians: For example, can we distinguish hepatitis type B and type C by clinical data; can a patient's fibrosis stage (one of five stages F0, F1, . . . , F4) be identified without performing a biopsy; and in which stage of viral hepatitis can interferon therapy be effective? In particular, we have developed data-mining methods that exploit the most valuable sources: the hepatitis database, the most well-known medical library MEDLINE (119,315 articles on hepatitis), and medical expert knowledge (Kawasaki, Nguyen, and Ho, 2003; Ho, Nguyen, et al., 2003).

Our framework consists of four iterative steps (Ho, Kawasaki, Takabayashi, and Nguyen, 2007):

1. Transform the original data by two temporal abstraction methods of APE (abstraction pattern extraction) and TRE (temporal relations extraction) into preprocessed datasets. The method APE maps a temporal sequence into one of predefined symbolic patterns describing possible hepatitis symptoms (Kawasaki et al., 2003; Ho, Nguyen, et al., 2003), while the method TRA detects the temporal

relations between basic abstracted patterns based on temporal logic (Ho, Kawasaki, et al., 2007).

2. Use D2MS and other learning methods, such as C5.0, random forest, and CN2-SD, to discover patterns and models from the preprocessed data sets.

3. Exploit MEDLINE for background or domain knowledge to support the knowledge evaluation.

4. Analyze the findings with (or by) physicians.

The main advantage of this framework is that the complexly structured temporal sequences are transformed into a set of simple representations within a medical context and thus increase the descriptive power of data mining. These enable us to apply many types of learning algorithms and their output conveys meaning to the physicians. In addition, the knowledge obtained from MEDLINE provides a key to focus on the search space and gives supportive and confident background on learned results, which prevents us from considering unlikely patterns.

Following are examples of discovered rules that were judged to be potentially new and useful for solving two problems:

R#2 (HCV): "TTT in high state with peaks" AFTER "ZTT in high state with peaks" (support count = 86, conf. = 0.73)

R#5 (HBV): "GOT in very high state with peaks" ENDS "GPT in extreme high state with peaks" (support count = 41, conf. = 0.71)

R#10 (NonLC): "GPT in very high state with peaks" AFTER "TTT in high state with peaks" AND "GOT in very high state with peaks" ENDS "GPT in very high with peaks" AND "GOT in very high state with peaks" AFTER "TTT in high state with peaks" (support count = 10, conf. = .80).

R#8 (LC): "GPT in very high state with peaks" AFTER "TTT in very high state with peaks" AND "GPT in very high state with peaks" BEFORE "TTT in high state with peaks" AND "GOT in very high state with peaks" AFTER "TTT in high state with peaks", (support count = 8, conf. = .80)

4.5.2   Mining Biological Data

Recent development in molecular biology has given the scientific community a large amount of "omics" data in genomics, proteomics, and metabolomics. These voluminous and precious data can effectively be used for medical and biological research only if one can extract functional insights from them. Bioinformatics methods are among the most powerful technologies available in life sciences today (Augen, 2005; Baldi and Brunak, 2001; Rashidi and Buehler, 2000; Wang, Zaki, Toivonen, and Shasha, 2004).

Working on mining biological data, we have established several learning-based computational methods for finding transcriptional regulatory rules (Pham, Clemente, Satou, and Ho, 2005), predicting beta and gamma turns in protein structure (Pham, Satou, and Ho, 2005), determining miRNA regulatory modules in human genome (Tran, Satou, and Ho, 2008), identifying acetylation and methylation areas in DNA sequences (Pham, Tran, Ho, Satou, and Valiente, 2005), and characterizing nucleosome dynamics (Le, Ho, and Tran, 2009).

We choose to briefly present here a work on knowledge discovery in protein network. It is well known that most proteins in cells are not independent individuals. Their permanent or transient interactions with other molecules, in particular other proteins in protein–protein interaction networks or in short protein networks, govern biological processes or biochemical events. There are three major research directions in protein networks related to data mining. First is predicting whether a given pair of proteins is interacting or not. Second is determining the features of protein from their networks such as their biological or biochemical or physiological features. Third is inferring the biological functions of interacting protein partners and of the protein networks as well (Ho, Nguyen, and Tran, 2007). It is also worth noting that the main trend of studying protein functions based on protein structure on the early days has changed to the trend of studying them based on protein networks.

Our method of predicting protein–protein interactions consists of two steps: (1) to extract relevant data in the form of ground facts from multiple genomic/proteomic databases, and (2) to employ inductive logic programming (ILP) to learn prediction rules from extracted data. There are available databases containing various kinds of protein information, and thus multiple sources may give us a chance to have as much as possible information about protein–protein interactions. The databases being extracted include UniProt (database of protein functions and structures, regions or sites of interest in the sequences, enzymes codes), InterPro (database of protein families, domains and functional sites), InterDom (database of protein interacting domains), Pfam (database of protein families), Prints (database of protein fingers), Gene Ontology, and Gene expression with totally nearly 275,000 extracted ground facts. ILP is one of the most effective classification techniques; it allows integrating diverse data types in terms of predicates. By running ILP on extracted ground facts we have detected various rules that allow predicting protein interactions with high values of sensitivity and specificity measures (Nguyen and Ho, 2008).

One interesting problem is that of predicting genes that cause diseases based on the protein interaction network and its relation to the gene network. There are several works on this important problem, all aiming to exploit the key assumption that a network-neighbor of a disease-causing gene is likely to cause either the same or a similar disease (Ideker and Sharan, 2008). Our proposed semisupervised learning method, which exploits protein networks learned from multiple sources, allows us to suggest more than 500 putative genes that have high potential of causing diseases (Nguyen and Ho, 2007).

4.5.3 Mining Materials Science Data

We addressed the following problem of mining materials science data in forward and inverse processes. In the former, a researcher postulates a crystal structure or a material formula and then predicts what properties that structure or formula will have. In the latter the researcher enters the properties they are looking for, and the mining system gives them a crystal structure or formula that is likely to have those properties. The inverse process cannot begin until the forward model is completed because the former depends on information in the model (Curtarolo et al., 2005).

Our goal was to find optimized structures of PtRu nano clusters adsorbed on carbon nanotubes (a promising catalyst for use in fuel cells) by combining data-mining methods and *ab initio* calculations on generated structures of PtRu nanoclusters adsorbed on carbon nanotubes. In fuel cell systems that use H_2 and O_2 gas as fuel, CO molecules are known to deactivate the catalytic function of the Pt bimetal catalysts. This deactivation process is called CO poison. A weaker binding of the CO molecule on a PtRu cluster may lead to a more efficient catalyst for fuel cells. Thus, finding the structure of PtRu nanoclusters adsorbed on carbon nanotubes that minimizes the CO adsorption energy is a significant task in nanocatalyst design.

Our method consists of two phases: (1) to generate a database of the structures of PtRu bimetal nanoclusters adsorbed on carbon nanotubes (with a size smaller than 1 nm), and (2) to find in this database the optimized structure of the PtRu bimetal nanoclusters adsorbed on carbon nanotubes that has the lowest CO adsorption energy (Nguyen, Sugiyama, Fujiwara, Mitani, and Dam, 2009).

In this subsection we have shown various examples of successful or ongoing projects on mining scientific data as well as the recent research directions in machine learning/data mining that offer advanced techniques to deal with complexly structured data; in this way we have tried to clarify some of the different opportunities and challenges in the very promising field of scientific data mining. See Figure 4.5.

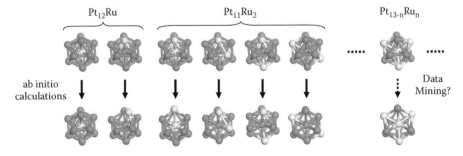

FIGURE 4.5
Construction of optimized structures of PtRu bimetal clusters.

4.6   Conclusion

In our view on knowledge science ingredients, information science essentially is about how machines can support humans in creating and using knowledge, of which knowledge discovery can be thought of as machine-based knowledge creation.

Back to the development of artificial intelligence, of which a critical problem is capturing knowledge from the experts. Many knowledge elicitation techniques might aid this process, but the fundamental problem remains: tacit knowledge that is normally implicit, inside the expert's head, must be externalized and made explicit. Knowledge acquisition (KA) has been well recognized as a bottleneck in the development of artificial intelligence. Traditionally, KA techniques can be grouped into three categories: manual, semiautomated (interactive), and automated (machine learning and data mining).

Fifteen years ago the *Encyclopedia of Artificial Intelligence* said, "Acquiring and modelling knowledge effectively can be the most time-consuming portion of the knowledge engineering process. Little methodology is practiced beyond unstructured interviewing. Automated methods are, for the most part, still in the research stage" (Shapiro, 1992, p. 719). Much has changed since that day. On one hand, various modeling methodologies and tools for KA have been constructed; for example, CommonKADS, a comprehensive methodology that covers the complete route of KA, is widely used by companies and educational institutions (Schreiber et al., 2000). On the other hand, the last two decades have witnessed much progress in machine learning research and applications (Bishop, 2006; Hastie, Tibshinari, and Friedman, 2008; Izenman, 2008) and in the emerging interdisciplinary field of knowledge discovery and data mining (Han and Kamber, 2006; Hand et al., 2001).

We are living in the most exciting of times with computer and computer networks. We have much more data around us than ever before. As data and knowledge have a strong relation as mentioned already, discovery of knowledge in data certainly plays day by day a more important role in knowledge science (Kriefgel, Borgwardt, Kroger, Pryakhin, Schubert, and Zimek, 2007).

5

Knowledge Synthesis

Jifa Gu

Chinese Academy of Sciences

CONTENTS

The most common knowledge can be acknowledged by the majority of people and used in most cases and times. However, due to the methods of getting data, information, and knowledge from different sources or inferring knowledge by using different mechanisms, under most circumstances, people will use different kinds of knowledge to express their own thoughts at first and through discussing and even debating with others may use synthesis to reach consensus. It means that some knowledge can be acknowledged only through the synthesis of thoughts. Then during the implementation in which people put the knowledge into practice, they have to use the synthesis of actions. This chapter introduces two methodologies: the meta-synthesis system approach (MSA); and the Wuli–Shili–Renli (WSR) system approach. The first one is useful for synthesis of thoughts, and the second one is useful for synthesis of actions. The chapter also introduces expert mining, which helps to uncover deep thought from an individual expert or group of experts. Finally, the chapter describes some case studies in the fields of economic, social, and human body systems.

5.1   Introduction

5.1.1   Various Definitions of Knowledge Synthesis

There are a lot of understandings and definitions of knowledge synthesis; here just a few are presented:

1. Knowledge syntheses—DARCOF* (Focus on agriculture): Knowledge synthesis analyzes, discusses, and synthesizes existing knowledge on an unclarified, and often disputed, subject in relation to the main points of view. This work takes place in a group of experts from different fields, which represent the different points of view on the subject. It is therefore important to include experts with different backgrounds and different perceptions of the subject. The Danish Research Centre for Organic Food and Farming (DARCOF) was established in 1995 as a so-called center without walls, where the actual research is performed in interdisciplinary collaboration among the participating research groups. The remit of DARCOF is to coordinate research for organic farming, with a view to achieving optimum benefit from the allocated resources. Its aim is to elucidate the ideas and problems faced in organic farming through the promotion of high-quality research of international standard.

2. Knowledge synthesis—CIET† (Focus on health): Knowledge synthesis is the aggregation of existing knowledge about a specific question by applying explicit and reproducible methods to identify, appraise, and then synthesize studies relevant to that question. The best-

---

* http://www.darcof.dk/about/knowledge.html
† http://www.ciet.org/en/documents/methods/200982517637.asp

known products of knowledge synthesis are systematic reviews and meta-analysis. CIET has also contributed to the development of a tool, called AMSTAR, for assessing the methodological quality of systematic reviews.

3. Knowledge synthesis—ZonMw* (Focus on health care): Knowledge synthesis is a strategy for combining information from research with information from policymakers and practitioners in a systematic and transparent way in order to promote the use of knowledge by disease prevention workers, health care providers and their professional associations, patients and patient groups, managers of health care and disease prevention institutions, health insurers, and policy makers. ZonMw is a partner in the European Commission-funded project Eurocan+Plus, launched to reduce the fragmentation in European cancer research.

4. Knowledge synthesis—a dictionary[†]: Based on the various concepts and different information from heterogeneous sources, knowledge synthesis is to integrate all in a consistent whole.

5. Knowledge synthesis—learning organization[‡] (Focus on organization): Knowledge synthesis is a social as well as an individual process. Sharing tacit knowledge requires individuals to share their personal beliefs about a situation with others. At that point of sharing, justification becomes public. Each individual is faced with the tremendous challenge of justifying his or her beliefs in front of others—and it is this need for justification, explanation, persuasion, and human connection that makes knowledge synthesis a highly fragile process. To bring personal knowledge into a social context, within which it can be amplified or further synthesized, it is necessary to have a field that provides a place in which individual perspectives are articulated, and conflicts are resolved in the formation of higher-level concepts.

6. Knowledge synthesis—Nakamori[§] (2008): Based on new systems thinking, a new systems approach to knowledge synthesis or construction has been developed as a systems methodology that consists of three fundamental parts: how to collect and synthesize knowledge, how to use our abilities in collecting knowledge, and how to justify the synthesized knowledge.

7. Intellectual synthesis—Wiki[¶] (Focus on intellectual synthesis): Intellectual synthesis is a broad term describing scholarly endeavors meant to unify and fuse a large amount of information into a single

---

[*] http://www.zonmw.nl/fileadmin/Nieuws_2007/10_oktober/knowledge_01.pdf
[†] http://tw.dictionary.yahoo.com/enterprise_content?p=Knowledge+synthesis
[‡] http://proceedings.informingscience.org/IS2003Proceedings/docs/138Vat.pdf
[§] http://www.igi-global.com/bookstore/article.aspx?Titled=41729
[¶] http://en.wikipedia.org/wiki/Intellectual_synthesis

integrated body of knowledge. Commonly, intellectual synthesis occurs as an interdisciplinary or multidisciplinary academic effort by one or more scholars.

5.1.2   Synthesis of Thoughts and Synthesis of Actions

Nonaka proposed the concept of knowledge synthesis, and recently he also mentioned the synthesis of thought and synthesis of action (Nonaka, Toyama, and Hirata, 2008). People use different kinds of knowledge to express their own thoughts at first, and through discussing and even debating with others they use synthesis to reach consensus. It means that some knowledge can be acknowledged only through the synthesis of thoughts. Then during the implementation in which people put the knowledge into practice, they have to use the synthesis of actions.

Here we introduce the following system methodologies for knowledge synthesis:

- MSA (Qian, Yu, and Dai, 1990)
- Shinayakana system approach (Sawaragi, Naito, and Nakamori, 1990)
- *i*-System (Nakamori, 2003)
- WSR system approach (Gu and Zhu, 1995; Gu and Tang, 2006)

The first two are useful for synthesis of thoughts, and the last two are useful for synthesis of actions.

Nakamori and his colleagues proposed a system approach for knowledge synthesis by using theory of knowledge construction, which consists of three parts: a knowledge integration model; the structure–agency–action paradigm; and the evolutionary constructive objectivism. The first one is a model of gathering and synthesizing knowledge; the second one relates to necessary abilities when gathering knowledge in individual domains; and the third one comprises a set of principles to evaluate and justify gathered and synthesized knowledge (Nakamori, 2009; Nakamori and Wierzbicki, 2010). We also introduce expert mining, which helps to uncover deep thought from individual expert or group of experts during synthesizing thoughts and actions. Finally, some case studies in the fields of environmental, economic, social, and human body systems will be described.

5.2   Meta-Synthesis System Approach

MSA is a Chinese system approach for solving problems related to the open, complex, and giant systems proposed by Qian et al. (1990) and Gu, Wang,

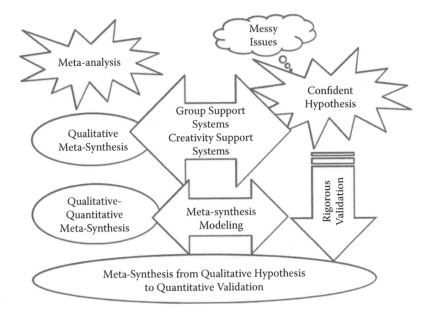

FIGURE 5.1
Contents of meta-synthesis. (From Tang, X.J. and Gu, J.F., *Proceedings of 45th Annual Conference of the International Society for the Systems Science*, Paper No. 01-093, Asilomar, CA, July 8–13, 2001.)

and Tang (2007). MSA stands for combining and synthesizing the data, information, models, and experts' experience and wisdom. MSA helps people use, discover, and create knowledge by combining it with computers.

There are three kinds of meta-synthesis (Figure 5.1):

1. Qualitative meta-synthesis
2. Qualitative and quantitative meta-synthesis
3. From qualitative to quantitative meta-synthesis

5.2.1 MSA Flowchart

For using the MSA to solve complex problems we design a flowchart:

Synchronous (meeting I) → Asynchronous (analysis) →
Synchronous (meeting II)

For solving economic decision-making problems we can use a more detailed flowchart that emphasizes various models used (Figure 5.2; Gu and Tang, 2003).

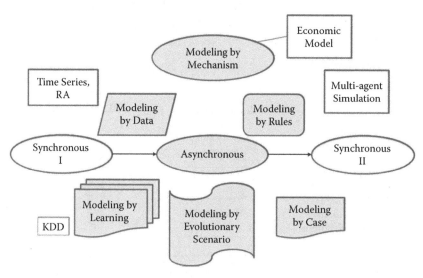

FIGURE 5.2
Flowchart of meta-synthesis approach.

5.2.2   Meta-Synthesis and Knowledge Science

The meta-synthesis approach helps convert tacit knowledge to explicit knowledge, helps acquire collective knowledge, and helps promote creating new knowledge.

5.3   Shinayakana Systems Approach

The Shinayakana* systems approach was proposed by Sawaragi and Nakamori (Sawaragi et al., 1990). This approach combines:

- Both hard and soft
- Interaction between analysts and computers
- Mathematics and adaptive formation of problem-solving process (adaptive learning, stimulation of intuition, and creativity within people)

During the process of implementation this approach keeps the so-called H^3 and I^3 principles:

- H^3: honesty, harmony, humanity
- I^3: interactive, intelligent, integration

This approach had been used in dealing with environmental problems.

---

* *Shinayakana* is a Japanese word meaning elastic, like a willow, but sharp, like a sword.

5.4 *i*-System

The *i*-system proposed by Nakamori (2003) is closely related to the Shinayakana system approach, but with many advancements used for knowledge creation and synthesis and with relation to the new concept of the creative space. This system introduces the knowledge pentagram system. The five ontological elements of the pentagram system are intelligence, involvement, imagination, intervention, and integration, which correspond to five diverse dimensions of the creative space (Figure 5.3).

5.5 **WSR System Approach**

The WSR system approach was proposed by Gu and Zhu (1995). It includes three aspects: Wuli (theory of "physics"), Shili (theory of managing affairs), and Renli (theory of dealing with people). The knowledge required in different *li*'s are natural science for Wuli, management science for Shili, and social science and humanity for Renli. Especially for Renli we need to consider and use logical thinking–emotion–benefit–morality–power (Gu, Tang, and Zhu, 2007).

Usually we use hard system thinking to convince people by logical argument, use humanity thinking to move people by emotion and feeling, use some soft system thinking with game theory to warn people by considering consequence and benefit, use education to educate people behaving by moral, and finally use critical system thinking to emancipate people from

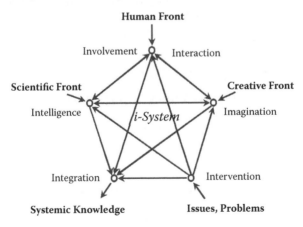

FIGURE 5.3
Pentagram system, or *i*-system.

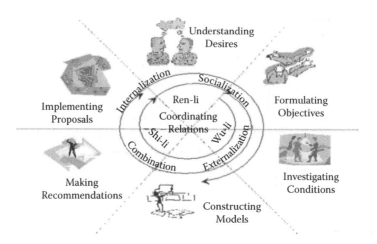

FIGURE 5.4
Working process for WSR approach.

wrong thinking and to force people by power. This approach stands for integrating three *li*'s in totality; thus, let us consider describing correctly, doing efficiently, and dealing with people effectively and actionable.

The modified version of the work process for the WSR approach is shown in Figure 5.4 (Tang and Gu, 2001).

5.6   Expert Mining

Expert mining is a new tool and method for mining the useful ideas and thoughts of the explicit and tacit knowledge from expert individually or group of experts collectively and synthetically.

5.6.1   From Data Mining to Expert Mining

There are many ways to expert mining, including the following:

1. From data mining to expert mining
2. From web mining to expertise-oriented search
3. From ontology-based approach to expert mining
4. From synthesizing experts' opinions to expert mining

We here give more descriptions for the fourth way. Dai, Yu, and Gu ran a large project under the support of National Natural Science Foundation of China titled "Man-Computer Cooperated HWME Supporting Macro-

Economy Decision-Making." One of the key problems in this project was how to synthesize the opinions (Gu, Tang, and Zhu, 2007). For this problem some members proposed the various methods for synthesizing the expert opinions, the concepts and theory of consensus building (Gu, 2004), and the tools for collecting, analyzing, and visualizing the expert's opinion—electronic common brain (ECB), group argumentation environment (GAE), and attributed directed graph model (Gu et al.; Tang and Liu, 2002). Especially in the Institute of Systems Science of the Chinese Academy of Sciences, Gu and Tang developed expert mining and ran a series of experiments.

5.6.2 Basic Concept for Expert Mining

Only some basic concepts are introduced here, such as how we define expert and how the experts express their opinions. Experts are considered people who may contribute their opinion, knowledge, and wisdom in solving problems. We may differentiate experts into different dimension, such as the number of experts, the degree of education, the title of job, the domain of knowledge, and the level of knowledge.

We also divide our experts into four classes: general people, expert, master, and guru (Figure 5.5). In the first class, each expert just looks like one sample in population. In this case we often use statistical methods and concern with experts' opinions only on trends and some simple statistics regarding some attributes in which we are interested. In the second class we care about the trends and some insights into their domain knowledge. In third class, we focus on the trends and more insight and not only on opinions they express explicitly but also their tacit background knowledge and their benefit delegated.

FIGURE 5.5
Experts in four classes.

The last class, gurus, contains great leaders, so we pay attention to their specific insights and wisdom. Expert mining collects not only experts' opinions expressed openly but also their unspoken thoughts. Usually experts express their knowledge and thoughts in several ways:

- Speak explicitly (language, word)—explicit
- Speak implicitly—tacit; express by gesture (expression in eyes, gesticulation, and tone)
- Speak on web—web
- Speak falsely (speak insincerely, false intelligence, rumor)—intelligence

In different cases we should use different methods and tools (see Gu, Song, Zhu, and Liu, 2009).

5.6.3   Expert Mining Methods

1. Meta-synthesis of opinions by text: There are three main methods for meta-synthesis of opinions by text: *simple survey (narrative), meta-analysis,* and *qualitative meta-synthesis.*
2. Meta-synthesis of opinions by meeting (ba, facilitation, mediation): We should consider the types of meeting: meeting for free discussion; meeting for deep research; meeting for making decision. In different meetings we design a different purpose and procedure and invite different kinds of experts, managers, and leaders. During organizing the meeting we should also consider following three aspects:
   a. Ba—for creating the friendly atmosphere that will help participants freely express their tacit knowledge (Nonaka, Toyama, and Konno, 2000)
   b. Facilitation—for organizing the meeting more smoothly and scientifically
   c. Mediation—for mediating the conflicts between participates with different benefits
3. Meta-synthesis of opinions by interview deeply: We can use psychology to mining some insights behind surface opinions.

5.6.4   Mining in Combination

For some complex problems we should combine different mining methods. The following six mining methods can be used:

1. Data mining: used to analyze a huge amount of data and to discover some useful knowledge
2. Web mining: used to extract useful information from; for example, the Internet or intranet

3. Text mining: used to extract some useful textual information from many texts in documents

4. Model mining: used to get results from; for example, calculations that are difficult for people to obtain using only their minds, forecasting models, and agent-based model simulation.

5. Psychology mining: used to dig the deep thoughts behind the surface of the mind

6. Expert mining: used to ask opinions and thoughts directly from experts. We ask experts to analyze all results that are sometimes contradicted with others and also to make final judgment for the obtained results. We also ask experts to create new ideas, methods, techniques and theories, and new alternatives for decisions, which means that we use wisdom to create something that originally did not exist.

Sometimes we use these mining methods in combination to solve social problems as shown in Figure 5.6 (Gu et al., 2009).

5.7 Meta-Synthesis Knowledge System

When trying to describe the knowledge system as a whole, Figure 5.7 is useful for combining and synthesizing the different knowledge and highlights

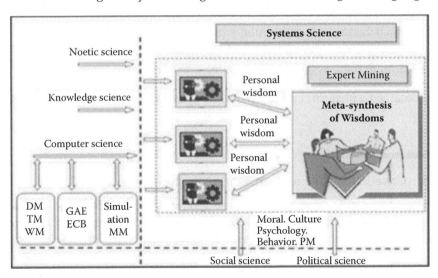

FIGURE 5.6
Six mining in combination.

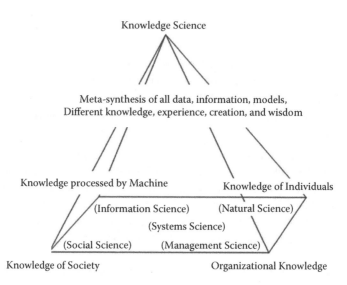

FIGURE 5.7
Knowledge science in total.

the meta-synthesis knowledge system. The following four systems are ways ideas in the meta-synthesis knowledge system can be used (Gu, 2001, 2008; Gu and Tang, 2007):

- Environmental system (data + model + expert)
- Economical system (data + information + model + knowledge + experience)
- Social system (data + opinion + mechanism [social physics] + model + experience + psychology)
- Human body system (text + mining + experience)

We designed a platform for meta-synthesis knowledge system (see Figure 5.8).

5.8　Case Study 1: Environmental System

The environmental system relates the following processes: basic production, production factor, waste, measure, environment change, environmental interaction, environmental impacts, and adjustment. Each process includes a lot of data and models, and all the processes and models are integrated. The Environment Agency of Japan proposed the environmental framework model (EFM) (see Figure 5.9), which mainly emphasizes the data and model integration. Nakamori and his colleagues tried to use the knowledge usually

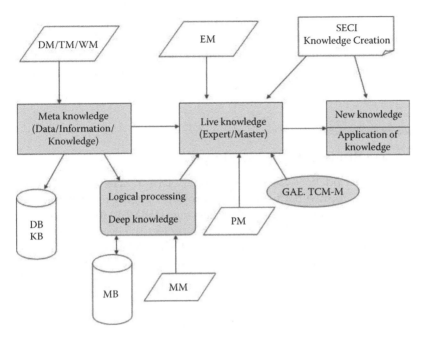

FIGURE 5.8
Meta-synthesis knowledge platform.

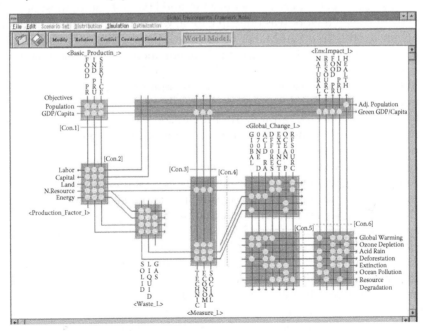

FIGURE 5.9
An environment framework model.

expressed by text language to understand some essential ideas behind users and the general population, so they proposed a so-called environment knowledge management system (EKMS). This EKMS uses both explicit and tacit knowledge to create new knowledge (Kawano and Nakamori, 2000).

5.9   Case Study 2: Economical System

During the period 1999–2003, the National Natural Sciences Foundation of China (NSFC) approved a 4-year major project engaging to implement a Hall of Workshop for Meta-Synthetic Engineering (HWMSE) for macroeconomic decision making (Grant 79990580). In this project the economic system was investigated. As examples, two test case studies related to forecasting the gross domestic product (GDP) growth rate were carried out using the MSA.

5.9.1   Forecasting GDP Growth Rate

This test was executed in the School of Knowledge Science at the Japan Advanced Institute of Science and Technology (JAIST) in January 2003. The aim of this test was to use the working process as shown in Figure 5.2 and to acquire some direct experience about MSA and HWMSE. Since most of computerized research work was done in China, we used only some of the tools available for this test. PathMaker by SkyMark Corporation was chosen as a cooperative support tool for our synchronous meeting. We also made full use of JAIST's advanced facilities, such as the specific collaboration room. To facilitate the formal discussion, several preparation meetings were held to introduce the knowledge and information related to the main topic of project: forecasting the GDP growth in China in 2003. The whole test procedure consisted of three phases: synchronous (rough) discussion, analysis, and synchronous (extensive) discussion.

Synchronous discussion about GDP growth—Meeting I: Here we ran (1) establishing meeting agenda, (2) idea generation, and (3) preliminary consensus. Then we ran some analyses: (1) forces review about GDP growth, (2) cause and effect analysis, and (3) consensus building.

Synchronous discussion about GDP growth—Meeting II: Participants were no longer only the experts as in Meeting I, and decision makers were also invited. In our test, the chair of Meeting I served as a decision maker in Meeting II. After analyzing, every participant of Meeting II made a prediction about the growth rate of China's GDP in 2003. Then we synthesized their opinions based on weighted sum method. When the same weight was given, the average of predictions given by all participants was 7.31%. When decision makers and general experts were given different weights, the weighted average of the predictions was 7.83%. When we increased the weight of decision maker four times, the final prediction result of GDP growth rate went up to 7.99%.

Comments on the test: The whole test lasted several days (January 14–January 21, 2003). Actually the preparation meeting took the longest time as a total of 9 hours. Meeting I took 3 hours, and Meeting II lasted 2 hours on separate days. From the test, three systems of HWMSE were clearly reflected. Initially, difficulties about machine system were underestimated until much time was invested. The role of expert system is critical toward further processing of discussion. We developed some collaborative tools for meeting in HWMSE, such as ECB and GAE that can support both Meeting I and II in our test. However, they needed further improvement and practical distributed applications at that time (Gu and Tang, 2003).

5.9.2 Forecasting GDP Growth Rate Under the Impact of SARS

In September 2004, we finished a test on discussing the impact on growth rate of GDP in China affected by severe acute respiratory syndrome (SARS) using MSA (Dai, Yu, and Gu, 2003; Gu, Wang, and Tang, 2007). We used the software PathMaker again as a main tool to run this test. We wanted to use the data, information, knowledge, models, expert opinions, and advanced computer technology organically to forecast the economic situation considering the impact of SARS.

We designed the meeting flowchart of MSA:

Synchronous Meeting I → Asynchronous analysis →
Synchronous Meeting II.

The flowchart of test was divided into the following steps:

M0 (preparation meeting)

M1-1 (Free discussion)

M1-2 (Topic discussion)

Brief summary

M1-3 (Further discussion)

Analysis; M2 (Detailed discussion)

In each step we assigned different tools provided by PathMaker to help the discussion and test. Connections were made to some other tools to facilitate the discussion, such as group argumentation environments, econometric models, neural network models, and data mining.

For discussion, opinions about GDP growth trends in 2003 were divided into three levels (low, medium, high) in consideration of three kinds of SARS impact (no impact, light impact, and heavy impact). Then nine scenarios about GDP growth in 2003 were acquired, and all participants were expected to study different scenarios by using different models provided for analysis. After all processes of testing, some conclusions were acquired. If participants or decision makers were not satisfied with this conclusion, the test process would be in iteration until some consensus or compromise was achieved. Certainly this test was running under some prerequisite and limited resources. We wish to extend this test to much more real situations.

This test was designed for a special session on meta-synthesis just after an IIASA* Workshop on Methodologies and Tools for Complex System Modeling and Integrated Policy Assessment held in IIASA during September 8–10, 2003. It took 5 hours on September 11, and eight experts invited by IIASA watched the demonstration and proposed much advice for further research.

5.10   Case Study 3: Social Harmony System

5.10.1   MBA Test—Discussion About Some Social Harmony Problems

In the beginning of July 2006, we ran a scientific test on discussing the social harmony problems by the expert mining, psychology mining, and model mining in an MBA course at the Chinese Academy of Sciences. We divided all MBA students into six groups to attend the discussion on six selected topics separately: (1) corruption, (2) housing, (3) health and insurance, (4) employment, (5) peasant workers, and (6) social safety. In each group we assigned one facilitator to use different discussion methods with some useful tools and methods, such as PathMaker, GAE, UciNet, GIS, interview, and game theory. Most of the participants were satisfied with such a new scientific discussion test.

Here we describe the discussion only on topic 2, housing; a detailed picture was given by Gu, Liu, and Song. At first they used PathMaker to collect and analyze opinions from experts (Figure 5.10). Based on these opinions the cause–effect chart for analyzing opinions was used (Figure 5.11). Then by using GAE they visualized the discussion process (Figure 5.12). Finally they tried to express opinions during discussing housing problem by network analysis (Figure 5.13). Through various discussions with the help of advanced information technology and tools, we synthesized the thoughts from all experts participated in this discussion. In topic 3 they applied psychology to uncover the ideas behind the experts' opinions (Figure 5.14) (Gu, Liu, and Song, 2007).

---

* International Institute for Applied Systems Analysis, Austria.

Topic II: Housing problem

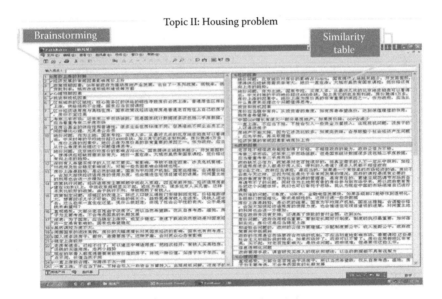

FIGURE 5.10
Using PathMaker to collect and analyze opinions from experts.

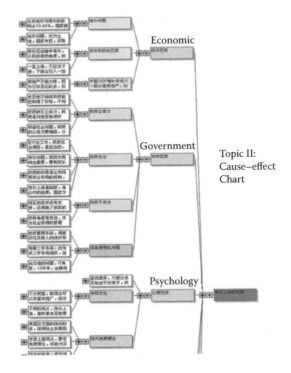

FIGURE 5.11
Cause–effect chart for analyzing opinions.

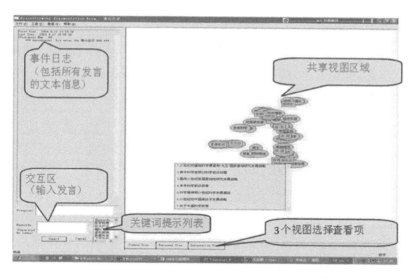

FIGURE 5.12
Common view for expressing different opinions within experts by GAE.

FIGURE 5.13
Expressing opinions during discussing housing problem by network analysis.

5.10.2 Taxi Driver

In one Chinese city, some taxi drivers were unsatisfied with the oil price rising and lack of subsidies from the local government. They stopped their business and waited for a good resolution. A research group from the Center

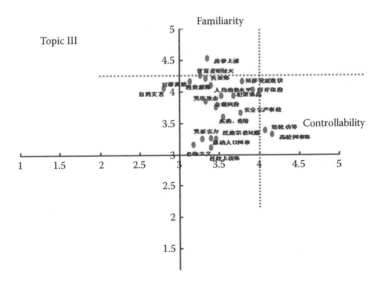

FIGURE 5.14
Expressing opinions by psychology.

of Interdisciplinary Study on Natural and Social Sciences ran a survey on these activities using a psychology method and analyzed the possibilities with a multiagent simulation.

Hypothetic condition (the process of modeling):

- We assumed the initial oil price equal to 5 RMB Yuan, which showed the tendency of gradually rising.
- We adjusted the unit price from 1.6 RMB Yuan per kilometer to 2 RMB Yuan per kilometer, which caused the passengers reducing and the rate of unload driving increasing. We assumed that when the unit price was 1.6 RMB Yuan per kilometer, the rate of unload driving was equal to 20%, which went up to 40% when the unit price was 2 RMB Yuan per kilometer.
- We canceled the subsidy of oil price, which means the taxi drivers' income would be reduced by 670 RMB Yuan per month.
- We embodied the taxi drivers' psychological change via reducing of their income.
- Different income levels of taxi drivers were given by the different degree of energy reducing.
- *Simulation experiment analysis*: Agents who owned the lower energy (income) stopped movement in 2 days, and the middle level of agents stopped in 3 days, while the high energy agents lasted 4 days. With more strict conditions, the agents would stop movement sooner.

This analysis could propose an effective perspective and way for decision makers to aid themselves to make practical and feasible policies, such as suitable taxi price adjustments to satisfy both the taxi companies and the taxi drivers (Liu et al., 2007).

5.10.3   ADVISE System

The ADVISE system was created in 2003 and ended in September 2007. It was developed by some U.S. research institutes and universities funded by the Department of Homeland Security. As a platform, this system uses data from different sources for analysis by data mining. Semantic web tools and methods to analyze and forecast the terrorists' information and event may provide some insight and enhance the semantics by knowledge use. It also uses visualization tools to help people to catch and understand some tacit knowledge (Figure 5.15 and Figure 5.16).*

In recent years we engaged in a large project supported by Ministry of Science and Technology and Administration Bureau of Traditional Chinese Medicine (TCM) in China. This project collected the academic thoughts and experiences from 100 Chinese masters in TCM based on information technology (IT) and databases. We analyzed these processed primary data further and got some theoretical and experimental results (Figure 5.17 and Figure 5.18).

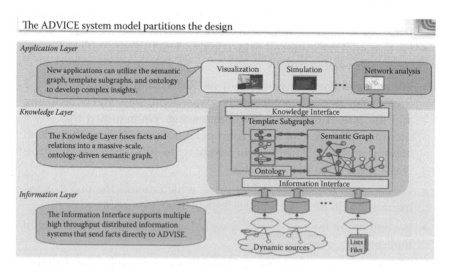

FIGURE 5.15
ADVISE system structure.

---

* Ryan Singel, Homeland Data Tool Needs Privacy Help, Report Says, March 20, 2007. http://www.wired.com/threatlevel/2007/03/homeland_data_t/#ixzz0ukxZUhNJ

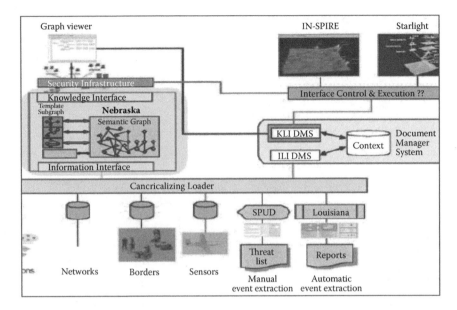

FIGURE 5.16
Architecture for ADVISE system.

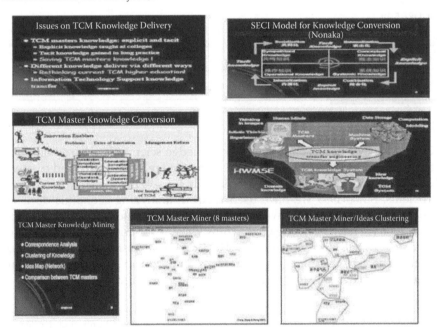

FIGURE 5.17
Traditional Chinese medicine knowledge mining. (From Tang, X.J., Zhang, N., and Wang, Z., *Computational Science—Proceedings of ICCS2007*, Part IV, also in Lecture Notes in Computer Science 4490, 35–42, Springer-Verlag, 2007.)

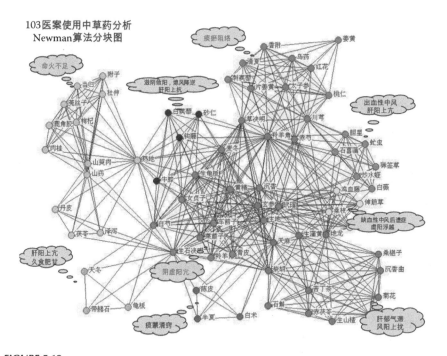

FIGURE 5.18
Research framework for mining knowledge in TCM. (From Gu, J.F., Song, W.Q., Zhu, Z.X., Gao, R., Liu YJ, *9th International Symposium on Knowledge and Systems Sciences* [KSS2008], Guangzhou, China, December 11–13.)

5.11   Conclusion

Knowledge synthesis is a branch of knowledge science. It is based on separate knowledge and makes synthesized knowledge more useful and creative. Knowledge synthesis is required especially for solving the complex system problems. Since 1999 we have used them in analyzing economic decision problems.* From 2004 we have tried to apply them to solve social problems. From 2006 we have been engaged in how we may inherit thoughts and experiences from selected past famous TCM doctors. We find that knowledge synthesis is very useful for us when we wish to collect knowledge from different experts in analyzing complex systemic problems.

* Most of the contents of this chapter are based on the following projects: (1) main project supported by NSFC (Grant 79990580) related to economic problems; (2) project under Eleven-Five state plan supported by Ministry of Science and Technology (2007BAI10B06-05) related to TCM; and (3) 973 operation project supported by the Ministry of Science and Technology (2010CB731405) related to social collective behaviors. The author also wishes to express gratitude to Prof. Niu Wenyuan and his research group in Interdisciplinary Center for Study of Natural and Social Sciences, Chinese Academy of Sciences for their support.

6

Knowledge Justification

Andrzej (Andrew) Piotr Wierzbicki

Poland National Institute of Telecommunication

CONTENTS

This chapter presents another perspective of viewing knowledge in technology and science: How do we interpret and substantiate or justify knowledge today? The chapter starts with what is *today* in the beginnings of the era of knowledge society; then it turns to what we mean by *knowledge* and *episteme*, the way of creating and justifying knowledge characteristic for a given era or cultural sphere. The chapter discusses the naturally circular, positive feedback type of knowledge creation and justification processes that, contrary to a tradition in philosophy, are not a paradox but a natural evolutionary phenomenon. It shows how we should look today at the processes of knowledge creation and the accepted methods of justifying knowledge. Finally, it briefly presents diverse spirals of knowledge creation and discusses the principles of developing a new episteme of the era of knowledge civilization.

6.1   Introduction: Human Constructed Knowledge

What is knowledge? This is a very difficult question (see Wierzbicki and Nakamori, 2006), discussed also in other chapters; there are many possible answers. For this chapter, however, we shall use the meaning of the word *knowledge* as information organized for a given purpose, while *information* is anything that allows us to distinguish order from chaos. This definition already suggests that knowledge is constructed (organized) by us, humans, for certain purposes.*

We should be careful, however: knowledge can be also organized genetically, by nature. Animals and plants have knowledge; how does human knowledge differ? The Far East Buddhist philosophy assumes that there should not be a great difference between human and natural knowledge—and this is a correct postulate. However, there is an obvious difference: humans use language to discuss, record, and inherit knowledge, whereas animals and plants use only genetic inheritance. We shall see later that this difference is not too great (as we shall discuss later, human intuition, the source of most new ideas, is very similar to inherited knowledge) although significant: humans have books and other records, today also computerized, that constitute an *intellectual heritage of humanity* and are a fundament of all new knowledge.

Western philosophy wondered deeply how human knowledge is at all possible but did it from an overly anthropocentric, antinaturalist position, self-strengthened by ostensible paradoxes of the relation of the nature and knowledge that we shall discuss in more detail later. This Western philosophy perspective was summarized by Richard Rorty (1980), who criticized the concept of human knowledge as a mirror of nature. This criticism is correct: Knowledge is constructed by us, humans, to be useful for certain purposes, such as a house is constructed by humans to be useful for certain purposes, and a house is not a mirror of nature.

However, human knowledge would be useless if it was not relevant in relation to nature (including in humans), and we represent here an evolutionary perspective: *Human knowledge evolved together with human civilizations, and the measure of fitness in this evolution was the civilization usefulness* (of course, broadly understood, including artistic values) *of knowledge.*

If all human knowledge is constructed by us, if it evolves together with human civilizations, then the relevant questions we discuss in this chapter are: *How does knowledge evolve? How do we justify knowledge, that is, check whether new knowledge is correct and useful? What is specific in knowledge justification in the new era after informational revolution?*

---

* Such purposes should be understood very generally, including the purpose of satisfying the curiosity of our minds as in an old Zen principle: "I know, and I am satisfied."

Before we address these questions, it is good to specify first our basic assumptions—axioms that we hold to be true, that constitute our *hermeneutical horizon* (see Król, 2007).

6.2 Fundamental Evolutionary Naturalism

Naturalism means the belief that humans are not alone in the world, that there exists another part of reality, called *nature*, containing material objects and living entities, and that human knowledge results from interactions with nature. The first part of this assumption is easy to test: If somebody does not believe that there exists nature with some universal properties, let her take a position against a hard wall and imagine, try to convince herself that the wall is not hard, is easy to penetrate. If she cannot convince herself, this means that there exists nature with some universal properties. If she can achieve such conviction, it is easy to test it by running ahead with closed eyes. The last part of this assumption—that human knowledge results from interactions with nature— is much more controversial, since much of the tradition of Western philosophy tried to disprove such assumption by using ostensible paradoxes of the relation of nature and knowledge, which we discuss after listing all assumptions.

Fundamental naturalism means a more subtle but deeper assumption that all other living entities in nature (e.g., plants, animals) are also knowing subjects creating knowledge for their own purposes. This aspect is natural for Far East, Buddhist philosophy but is absent from most of Western philosophy that since Plato (see, e.g., the last part of *Timaios* in *Dialogues*, 380 BC) assumed the domination of humans over nature and since Immanuel Kant asked the question how human knowledge is possible without asking first how knowledge is constructed by plants or animals.

Fundamental evolutionary naturalism means combining the aforementioned assumptions with the belief that all nature, together with human societies and civilizations, evolves with time, following certain rules of evolution. These rules do not mean simple survival of the fittest individuals—which is a gross oversimplification of evolutionary development—but they include the preservation of such features of living entities or of groups of them (human civilizations evolved in groups of people) that increase their fitness and are useful for future developments. Fundamental evolutionary naturalism is not equivalent to atheism,* it is consistent with Buddhist religion or with the interpretation of Christian religion by St. Francisco.

---

* If God was the creator (Buddhism maintains that such an assumption is not necessary, that the world was not created, and that God can be interpreted as an ultimate goal), why should God bother about creating every single micro-organism when such excellent mechanism as evolution was available? The argument of creationists that evolution could not create irreducible complexity is wrong, because civilization evolution during the last 100 years has created irreducible complexity—software emerging out of hardware and irreducible to hardware.

Now we can turn to the discussion of the main reservation against naturalism—the arguments of Western philosophy that the relation of nature and knowledge apparently contains contradictions. This was best summarized by Leszek Kołakowski, who in his *Metaphysical Horror* (Kołakowski, 1988) says that it is known (in Western philosophy) since ancient Greek skepticism that all (naturalist) epistemology leads inevitably to paradoxes: of *infinite regress,* or a *vicious circle,* or an irreducible paradox of *self-reference.* This opinion was repeated by many philosophers of the 20th century, from Ludwig von Wittgenstein (1922, 1969) to Bruno Latour (1987), who formulated the following paradox of self-reference: "Since the settlement of a controversy is *the cause* of Nature's representation not *the consequence, we can never use the outcome*—Nature—to explain how and why a controversy has been settled" (p. 99).

However, disproving something through *reduction ad absurdum*—showing that this something leads to paradoxes—is dangerous logically, because it relies on the exclusion of the middle. Thus, if somebody shows that there is a third way, paradoxes vanish. That happened with the paradox of ancient Greek skepticisms that Achilles could never overtake a turtle—because if Achilles comes to the point where the turtle is presently, the turtle manages to come a small way forward in an infinite regress. This paradox ceased to be paradoxical when mathematicians in the time of Descartes proved that there is a third way: an infinite series can have a finite limit.

The point is that information technology and systems science proved during the 20th century that infinite regress, vicious circle, and self-reference are not paradoxes if they are treated as dynamic phenomena. In fact, self-reference (called positive feedback,* but it is the same phenomenon) is used as the basic principle in flip-flop elements necessary for computer memories, used now in billions of exemplars around the world. Infinite regress (called negative feedback, but again it is the same phenomenon) is applied in automatic regulation (e.g., of the arms of robots) used now in industry worldwide. If infinite regress and self-reference are paradoxes, then robots and computers cannot function; if they do function, infinite regress and self-reference are not paradoxes anymore. If a vicious circle concerns static, binary logic, it is obviously a paradox, but what obliges us to use static binary logic for the description of knowledge creation and justification processes that are obviously dynamic and often admit a third way? All this shows that Latour (1987), stating that the outcome cannot be the cause, overlooks the third possibility: that they can be both causes and outcomes in a feedback

---

* Feedback is a circular impact of a time stream of consequences on the time stream of causes, obviously in a dynamic sense, with some delay (otherwise it would be truly a paradox); because it concerns entire time streams, it relies on infinite regress. If the consequences support the causes, as in self-reference, the feedback is called positive and leads either to avalanche-like growth or, in nonlinear systems with constraints, to flip-flop behavior. If the consequences counteract the causes, as in control of robotic arms, the feedback is called negative or stabilizing.

loop, as in automatic control or in computer technology. Thus, the arguments of Western philosophy against naturalism are based on inadequate logic,* paradoxes that turned out to be quite natural phenomena.

This is only one example showing how the development of science and technology also changes the validity of a very basic reasoning. It also shows that knowledge justification is historically changing. We shall use here, therefore, the concept of an *episteme* in an extended sense of Michel Foucault (1972). In ancient Greek, *episteme* meant entire rational knowledge; Foucault has shown that the way of creating and justifying knowledge is characteristic for a given historical era and called it *episteme*—using examples from the past pre-industrial era of forming capitalism and the industrial civilization or modern era. We just extend the concept of an *episteme*, in the Foucault sense of *a specific way of creating and justifying knowledge,* also to a future civilization era (say, the era of knowledge civilization or however we shall call the era after informational revolution) and also to specific civilizations of the world (say, Western versus Far East) as well as to specific cultural spheres that might differ in this respect. The episteme of the era after information revolution is not formed yet, but we can postulate that it should be a synthesis of diverse partial episteme, including that of Western and Far East civilizations; for this reason, we believe that fundamental evolutionary naturalism might be the basis of such synthesis.

Therefore, we present here a general model of knowledge creation and justification in a spiral, positive feedback form (which obviously is based on self-reference and infinite regress), consistent with fundamental evolutionary naturalism (Figure 6.1).

The spiral can start at any point, but let us start with the node *Heritage Knowledge,* which represents intellectual heritage of humanity. Through a transition called *Enlightenment* (which has many other names: *abduction, illumination, eureka, aha,* the phenomenon of having an idea that is deeply intuitive; discussed in more detail later), *New Theories and Tools* are created. These theories and tools must be somehow justified and evaluated; those that are valuable pass to the *Heritage Knowledge.* The basic way of testing them, however, is their *Application* to *Existing Reality* (containing, e.g., nature, human societies, artifacts) to obtain selected goals in *Modified Reality;* through a *Recourse* modified reality becomes existing one. People make *Observations* of *Modified Reality* and draw conclusions about the place that *New Theories and Tools* should have in the *Heritage Knowledge.*

---

* Logic must be adequate to its field of applications. In the 20th century, multivalued logic was developed first by Jan Łukasiewicz (1911), then as fuzzy set theory by Lofti Zadeh (1965) and many others, then as rough set theory by Zdzisław Pawlak (1991); meanwhile, temporal logic concerning phenomena such as dynamic feedback theory was also developed. The philosophical arguments discussed above are based on classical binary logic, static, and with excluded middle ("there is no third way"), while at least three-valued, temporal logic of feedback phenomena is needed in that case.

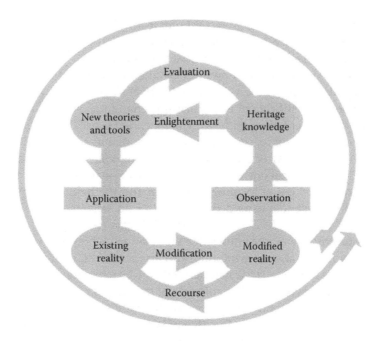

FIGURE 6.1

A general spiral OEAM of evolutionary knowledge creation and justification. (Wierzbicki, A.P., Kameoka, A., & Nakamori, Y., in *Futurology: The Challenge of the XXI Century* (A. Kukliński & K. Pawłowski, Eds.), 45–82, 2008.)

The entire spiral is repeated in an infinite regress, the heritage knowledge is accumulated, increased through a positive feedback; the result is avalanche-like growth of knowledge. In such a spiral, according to fundamental evolutionary naturalism, there is no sense to ask for an ultimate foundation of knowledge; we can at most ask about ultimate goal. However, every avalanche-like growth might be dangerous if unchecked. Therefore, stabilizing negative feedbacks are necessary. Such feedback might be provided by *Evaluation,* if we apply rigorous ways of knowledge justification and evaluation. Unfortunately, opinions about the question, *what is a correct way of knowledge justification and evaluation,* developed divergently during last century.

6.3   The Episteme of Three Different Cultural Spheres

Michel Foucault (1972) showed that an episteme in his sense is relatively durable during an era of civilization; using a later concept contributed by Fernand Braudel (1979), we can say that an episteme is a historical *long duration structure.* However, the work of Foucault was already contributing to postmodernism, a sign of dissolution of the modern episteme of industrial civilization, while the process of destruction of that episteme started much earlier—say, with the relativism of Albert Einstein (1905), the indeterminism of Werner Heisenberg (1927), the incompleteness of truth in mathematics of Kurt Gödel (1931), and the critique of empirical logicism of Willard V. O. Quine (1953/1964). The development of information technology added another dimension: while C. P. Snow (1960) wrote about *two cultures* (meaning, in fact, the differing episteme of natural and social sciences), toward the end of the 20th century we could observe a divergent development of differing ways of constructing and justifying knowledge or of differing *episteme of three cultural spheres* (see Wierzbicki, 2007):

- Basic, hard and natural sciences
- Social sciences and humanities
- Technology

We should clarify first what we understand by the word *technology*. It means diverse things to diverse people. For a postmodern social scientist, it might mean an autonomous force enslaving humanity. For an economist, it might mean a way of doing things, a technical process. In common language, it might mean a technical artifact. And for a natural scientist, it might mean an application of scientific theories.

For a technologist, though, it might mean the art of constructing tools, an inherent faculty of humanity, motivated by the joy of creation; liberating people from hard work; helping technology brokers (e.g., venture capitalists, bankers, managers) make money—and if this is enslaving, the brokers are responsible; and stimulating the development of hard science by inventions that provide new principles to develop new concepts. This meaning is referred to as *technology proper*—how a technologist understands technology—or *techne*, an ancient Greek word meaning the art of creating artifacts and tools. Actually, *techne* changes (similar to *episteme*) together with civilization eras: It was different in time of stone tools, different for bronze tools, different in industrial civilization; it is different in time after information revolution.

These various meanings of technology indicate that the differences in hermeneutical horizons of these three cultural spheres might have grown very deep at the end of the 20th century. But most important are the differences in justifying and evaluating knowledge.

Even while a hard or natural scientist knows that all knowledge is constructed by creating models and that there is no absolute truth or objectivity, she believes that scientific theories are laws of nature discovered by humans; only a few hard scientists would call them models of knowledge created by humans. A hard scientists values truth and objectivity as ultimate ideals; metaphorically, the *hard scientist resembles a priest*. However, most important is the *paradigmatic method* of knowledge justification and evaluation applied by a hard or natural scientist, described by Thomas Kuhn (1962). A hard or natural scientist compares every new idea, new element of a theory, or new experimental facts with an *exemplar theory* of her field and accepts them if they fit or enlarge this basic theory or rejects them if they do not fit; this way, she *defends the paradigm* of the field of science. First when new ideas amass and are supported by empirical facts not fitting into the old paradigm, it might come to a *scientific revolution* (e.g., the relativity theory or quantum theory revolutions in physics). Hence, most important in justifying new knowledge in hard and natural sciences is its consistence with human intellectual heritage; consistence with empirical facts is also important but secondary. Moreover, we know from Werner Heisenberg's (1927) paper that there are no absolute empirical facts, because the very act of measurement distorts the measured variable; later, it was added that measurements are theory dependent, but this depends on the field of applications.

A postmodern social scientist or a soft scientist believes that all knowledge is subjective, constructed, negotiated, relativist, is a result of a social discourse. Metaphorically, a *postmodern social scientist resembles a journalist:* anything goes as long it is interesting. There are traps in such an episteme, which would not stand up against a serious Kantian-type internal critique (when applied reflexively to sociology, such a belief would lead to the conclusion that sociology is a social discourse about itself). Therefore, not all social scientists and humanists today follow postmodernism that might be regarded as an intellectual fashion at the end of the industrial civilization era. Generally, however, because of the difficulties in social sciences and humanities with obtaining empirical data and tests, these sciences developed special techniques of knowledge justification. They use the paradigmatic method but are enhanced by two other essential techniques. One is *hermeneutics*, meaning achieving understanding of certain phenomena (e.g., past historical events) by intuitive comparison with human intellectual heritage in a given field. Another is *discourse*, meaning social debate and critique of new theories and postulates. Although mostly stressed by social sciences and humanities (e.g., some specialists define humanities as hermeneutic sciences), hermeneutics and discourse are in fact also used by natural sciences and by technology.

A technologist is much more relativist and pragmatic in her episteme than a hard natural scientist—and much more demanding in requirements of knowledge justification than a social scientist. She readily agrees that scientific theories are models of knowledge because, if she has several competing theories, she simply compares their usefulness. But she requires that these theories should be as objective as possible, tested in practice, and she demands that they should be *falsifiable. Falsification* is a method of knowledge justification proposed by Karl Popper (1934, 1972) to escape the logical inadequacy of a classical method of justification called *induction**; according to Popper, a theory might be distinguished from ideology if it is *falsifiable*, that is, admits empirical tests that might disprove the theory (so called *crucial* or *critical experiments*); a theory is more reliable if it has passed more unsuccessful attempts to disprove it. While the falsification method of Popper was not accepted by science (particularly by postmodern social science that ridicules falsification, possibly because it is almost impossible to construct critical experiments in social sciences) and was replaced by paradigmatic knowledge justification, it is in fact practiced by technology. Technology relies on critical experiments to test the safety of new tools (e.g., crash tests of new cars) or the durability of other artifacts. Thus, technology relies on falsification†—a quite different method of knowledge justification than the paradigmatic method.

Whatever scientists might believe, technology is not a mere application of scientific theories. Technology uses scientific theories but is not paradigmatic about these theories. If a technologist does not have scientific theories to rely upon, she will not agree to wait until such theories are created but will try to solve the problem anyway using her own creativity. There are many examples when technological progress was ahead of existing scientific theories—from the construction of the wheel to the telescope that preceded optics to the feedback controller used by James Watt over 100 years before full feedback theory was developed to the quasi-random number generator in digital computers invented about 20 years before the theory of deterministic chaos was developed. Metaphorically, a *technologist resembles an artist.* She also values tradition like an artist does, much more than a scientist: An old car is beautiful and, if well cared for, can become a classic.

As discussed already, technology and technological science are closest to Popperian falsificationism; hard science is rather paradigmatic in the sense of Thomas Kuhn, while postmodernist social science is also paradigmatic and ridicules falsificationism as another relict of positivism (although Karl Popper advanced it actually as an argument against positivism). With all

---

* Classical philosophy (even until today) maintained that science develops by induction; that is, by observing many repeated instances of certain phenomena and deriving general conclusions from these observations. Karl Popper pointed out that this is logically insufficient (induction is admissible in mathematics, when it might be complete, that is, proven to be repeated ad infinitum; in natural sciences, the induction is always incomplete: how many times should a phenomenon be repeated until we are certain?). Thus, Popper postulated that we develop new theories by intuition; it is only important that there should be enough attempts to falsify every new theory.

† It is ironic that Karl Popper himself (who was a mathematician and theoretical physicist and understood technology as a mere application of scientific theories) believed that falsification is not used in technology (1956), because supposedly technology does not use critical experiments and does not abandon theories after disproving them. But much intellectual effort in technology goes to the design of critical tests, and many new designs of tools or artifacts are abandoned when they do not pass critical tests. Moreover, Rachel Laudan (1984) tried to find signs of paradigmatic method and scientific revolutions in technology and admitted that such signs are impossible to find, because technology is more pragmatic than paradigmatic.

these fundamental differences we must, however, observe that all these three cultural spheres might have important contributions to methods of knowledge justification. Beside the basic distinction between the paradigmatic and falsificationist method, three ways of knowledge justification are basic for knowledge development (at least in academia and at universities):

- Debate and discourse
- Hermeneutic understanding
- Experimental design and testing

All of them require intuitive idea formation (e.g., an idea how to design a good experiment is sometimes as difficult to generate as a new theory). Therefore, before describing them in more detail, we turn first to a naturalist and evolutionary, rational theory of intuition.

6.4   Powerful but Natural and Fallible Intuition

Since Plato (380 BC) until the 19th century, Western philosophy treated intuition as proof that human thought is capable of deep and infallible abstraction. Plato illustrated this in the story of how Socrates asked a young slave (an uneducated man in Greek society) to solve the problem of how to construct two equal squares out of one square; guided by Socrates, the slave solved the problem, which according to Plato proved that people are capable of forming deep ideas by intuition. However, the slave might be a carpenter, and the problem would be trivial for him: Cut the square by its diagonals into four triangles, and glue the triangles pairwise into two smaller squares.*

Until non-Euclidean geometry was discovered in the 19th century, philosophy treated intuition as proof that the human mind can produce infallible knowledge. Immanuel Kant (1781) distinguished this type of knowledge as *a priori synthetic judgments*. Earlier, Locke (1690) wrote, "And this I think we may call intuitive knowledge. For in this the mind is at no pains of proving or examining, but perceives the truth as the eye doth light, only by being directed towards it. Thus the mind perceives that white is not black, that a circle is not a triangle, that three are more than two and equal to one and two. Such kinds of truths the mind perceives at the first sight of the ideas together, by bare intuition; without the intervention of any other idea; and this kind of knowledge is the clearest and *most certain* that human frailty is capable of." The point is, however, that *we know today that all examples given by*

---

* When I quoted his solution to a philosopher of mathematics, he was deeply annoyed: "It is not a mathematical proof!" The point is that it is a solution to that problem, [only not just from a mathematical perspective but also from a technical perspective].

Locke are only relative truths; a circle is topologically equivalent to a triangle, one and two modulo two is one and less than two, and so forth.

This has created difficulties for contemporary philosophy, which has tried to address intuition from diverse perspectives. The discovery of non-Euclidean spaces in the 19th century and later generally the relativism of knowledge, recognized in the 20th century, has led to considerable scepticism about such interpretations and thus generally about the value of intuition (see, e.g., Bunge, 1962). The role of intuition remained extremely important in mathematics and even in the 20th century was stressed by such thinkers as Poincare, Brouwer, or Gödel. Nevertheless, philosophical reflection on intuition in the 20th century—as represented by Bergson (1903) or later by Polanyi (1966) with his concept of tacit knowing, practically equivalent to experiential knowledge thus including both emotions and intuition—attached great importance to intuitive reasoning but treated it as a mystic force and refused to analyze it in rational terms. Another part of philosophy refused even to speak about intuition, as stressed by Wittgenstein (1922), who said in his famous quotation, "Wovon man nicht sprechen kann, darüber muss man schweigen" (loosely translated, "if we cannot speak about it, we must remain silent")—meaning that we should not analyze metaphysical concepts, including such concepts as intuition. This conviction became popular among natural sciences in the 20th century, where the term *intuitive* became almost equivalent to *nonscientific.* However, intuition is a powerful source of ideas, and we must understand it correctly.

Thus, what is intuition? Is it a supernatural ability of human mind distinguishing it from animals and producing infallible truths, or is it rather a very powerful but natural ability, common with animals, producing new ideas but such that require justification and evaluation? We shall show that the second opinion is true and can be explained by a rational, naturalistic, and evolutionary theory of intuition.

By *rational theory* we understand here a theory rationally derived from reasonable assumptions, close to Quine (1953) and Popper (1972): a theory is rational, if it can be deductively derived from some abstract principles, but it is also empirically viable and can be falsified with the help of an experiment or at least allows for practical conclusions that can be tested. In everyday language, we tend to use the word *intuitive* with some connotation of *irrational.* We do not want to make intuition rational; we want to explain its functioning only in rational, naturalistic terms.

The first element of the rational theory of intuition is based on contemporary knowledge—from the field of computational complexity and telecommunications—about relative complexity of processing video and audio signals. The ratio of bandwidth necessary for transmitting video and audio signals is at least 100:1 (at least 2 MHz to at most 20 kHz). Let us assume conservatively—to obtain a lower bound estimate—the simplest and one of the mildest of nonlinear increases in computational complexity, say, the quadratic increase of complexity of a given type of processing problem with the number of data processed. Then we obtain the ratio of computational complexity of processing video and audio signals at least 10,000:1. Thus, the old proverb *A picture is worth a thousand words* is not quite correct: *A picture is worth at least ten thousand words.*

The second element of this theory is a *dual thought experiment*. In this experiment, we consider the question: How did people process the signals from our environment just before the evolutionary discovery of speech? They had to process signals from all our senses holistically, though dominant in received information was the sense of sight. Yet they were able to overcome this difficulty and developed evolutionary a brain containing 10^{11}–10^{12} neurons. We still do not know how we use full potential of our brain, but it was needed evolutionarily. We know that the brain processes signals with a great degree of parallelism and distribution, certainly uses neuron networks (though much more complicated than contemporary artificial neural networks), and in a holistic processing of signals uses multivalued rather than binary logic. Biological research on real neurons shows that an appropriate model of a neuron should be dynamic and nonlinear, with extremely complex behavior. Thus, to model a neuron well we would need the computational capability of a contemporary personal computer, not a single digital switch or a sigmoid function (the latter being used in contemporary artificial neural networks to represent a single neuron).

Reflecting on the dual thought experiment we realize that the discovery of speech was an excellent evolutionary shortcut. It turned out that we could process signals 10^4 times simpler. This enabled the intergenerational transfer of information and knowledge; we started to build up the cultural and intellectual heritage of mankind, the *third world* of Popper (1972). The biological evolution of people slowed down (some biologists say that it actually stopped), especially the evolution of our brains, but we accelerated intellectual and civilization evolution. Many biologists wonder *why* our biological evolution has stopped. We think that the dual thought experiment described here gives a convincing theory why it happened.

This development had also disadvantages. Seeking better ways of convincing other people, we devised binary logic and excluded the middle. Binary logic also contributed of course to tremendous civilization achievements—the construction of computers and computer networks—but it still biases our way of understanding the world. The best example of this bias is *cognitivism*, or the conviction that all cognitive processes (e.g., perception, memory, learning) are based on a language-like medium, on a *language of thought* (see, e.g., Fodor, 1994; Springer and Deutsch, 1981), and thus functioning of the mind can be modeled as the functioning of a giant computer. Note that cognitivism is a simplification to the same degree as language is a simplification of the original capabilities of our mind.

If any language is only a code, simplifying the processing of information about the real world about 10^4 times, than each word, out of necessity, must have many meanings, and to clarify our meaning we have to devise new words. By multiplying words, we gradually describe the world more precisely, but we discover more quickly new aspects of an infinitely complex world (e.g., the *microcosmic* or *macrocosmic* aspects; see Vollmer, 1984) than we succeed in creating new words.

If our knowledge must be expressed in language, if only for interpersonal verification, and language is only an imperfect code, then an absolutely exact, objective knowledge is not possible—not because human knowing subject is imperfect but because she uses imperfect tools for creating knowledge, starting with language. The fact that language is only a very imperfect tool for describing reality was not seriously considered by the entire philosophy of the 20th century that concentrated on language—starting with logical empiricism and ending with cognitivism, constructivism, and postmodernism.

However, do we still use our original capabilities of holistic processing of signals—let us call them *preverbal*, since we had them before the discovery of speech? The discovery of speech stopped the development of these abilities and pushed them to the subconscious or unconscious. Our conscious ego, at least its analytical and logical part, identified itself with speech, verbal articulation. Because the processing of words is 10^4 times simpler, our verbal, logical, analytical, conscious reasoning uses only a small part of the tremendous capacity of our brain that was developed before the discovery of speech. However, the capabilities of preverbal processing remained with us—*and can be called intuition,* although we do not always know how to rationally use them.

Let us define intuition as the ability of preverbal, holistic, subconscious (or unconscious, or quasi-conscious)* processing of sensory signals and memory content, left historically from the preverbal stage of human evolution. Let us call this definition an evolutionary rational definition of intuition. Let us conclude that intuitive abilities should be associated to a considerable part of the brain. Then should this be noted in the research on the structure of brain, on neurosurgery?

And it was noted, for example, by the voluminous results of the hemispherical asymmetry of the brain (see, e.g., Springer and Deutsch, 1981). These results suggest that a typical left hemisphere (for right-handed people; for left-handed we can observe the reverse role of brain hemispheres) is responsible for *verbal, sequential, temporal, analytical, logical, rational* thinking, while a typical right hemisphere is responsible for *nonverbal, visual, spatial, simultaneous, analog, intuitive* thinking. Thus, Young (1983) defined intuition as the activity of the right hemisphere of the brain. However, Young's definition does not lead to a rational theory, because we cannot conclude from it, for example, how to stimulate and better use intuition. On the other hand,

---

* Quasi-conscious action can be defined as an action we are aware of doing but do not concentrate our conscious abilities on it; we perform many quasi-conscious actions, such as walking and driving a car.

we can draw such conclusions, among diverse others, from the evolutionary rational definition of intuition.

To illustrate such diverse possibilities let us note the following conclusion: Memory related to intuitive thinking should have different properties than memory related to rational thinking. And it has: Modern research on the functioning of memory (see, e.g., Walker, Brakefield, Morgan, Hobson, and Stickgold, 2003) shows that the phase of deep memorization occurs during sleep, when our consciousness is switched off.

We should further note that all people make many intuitive decisions of quasi-conscious, operational, repetitive character. These are learned decisions: when walking, a mature person does not have to articulate (even mentally) the will to make the next step. These quasi-conscious *intuitive operational decisions* are such simple and universal that we do not attach any importance to them. But we should study them to better understand intuition. Note that their quality depends on the level of experience. We rely on our operational intuition if we feel well trained. Dreyfus and Dreyfus (1986) show experimentally that the way of decision making depends critically on the level of experience: It is analytical for beginners and deliberative or intuitive for masters.

Now there comes a critical question: Does consciousness help or interfere with good use of master abilities? If intuition is the old way of processing information, suppressed by verbal consciousness, then the use of master abilities must be easier after switching off consciousness. This theoretical conclusion from the evolutionary rational definition of intuition is confirmed by practice. Each athlete knows how important it is to concentrate before competition. The best concentration can be achieved by, for example, Zen meditation practices, which was used by Korean archers before winning the Olympic competition.

We contend that this theoretical conclusion is also applicable for creative decisions, such as scientific knowledge creation, formulating and proving mathematical theorems, and new artistic concepts. Creative decisions are in a sense similar to strategic political or business decisions. They are usually nonrepetitive, one-time decisions. They are usually deliberative—based on an attempt to reflect on the whole available knowledge and information. They have often been accompanied by an enlightenment effect (eureka or aha effect), suddenly having an idea.

Before describing a model of a creative intuitive decision process, let us recall that Simon (1957) defined the essential phases of an analytical decision process to be *intelligence, design, and choice;* later another essential phase, *implementation,* was added (Lewandowski and Wierzbicki, 1989). For creative or strategic intuitive decision processes, a different model of their phases was proposed in Wierzbicki (1997):

> *Recognition,* which often starts with a subconscious feeling of uneasiness. This feeling is sometimes followed by a conscious identification of the type of the problem.

Deliberation or analysis; for experts, a deep thought deliberation suffices, as suggested by Dreyfus and Dreyfus (1986). Otherwise an analytical decision process is useful—with intelligence and design but suspending the final elements of choice.

Gestation; this is an extremely important phase; we must have time for forgetting the problem to let our subconscious work on it.

Enlightenment (called also *abduction, illumination, aha, eureka effect*); the expected eureka effect might come but not be consciously noticed; for example, after a night sleep it is simply easier to generate new ideas (which is one of the reasons group decision and brainstorming sessions are more effective if they last at least 2 days).

Rationalization. To communicate our decision to others we must formulate verbally, logically, rationally our reasons. This phase can be sometimes omitted if we implement the decision ourselves.*

Implementation, which might be conscious, after rationalization, or immediate and even subconscious.

Especially important are the phases of gestation and enlightenment. Their possible mechanism relies on trying to use the enormous potential of our mind on the level of preverbal processing: If not bothered by conscious thought, the mind might turn to a task specified before as the most important but forgotten by the conscious ego. There exist cultural institutions supporting gestation and enlightenment. The advice of emptying your mind, concentrating on void or on beauty, and forgetting the prejudices of an expert through Japanese Zen meditation or a tea ceremony is precisely a useful device for allowing our subconscious mind to work.

If we consider that intuition is mostly acquired by lifelong learning and is preverbal, then it is almost equivalent to the tacit knowing introduced by Polanyi (1966) and stressed as tacit knowledge by Nonaka and Takeuchi (1995). However, the evolutionary rational definition of intuition discussed here allows us also to better understand diverse aspects of tacit knowledge and has a strong explanatory power.

To illustrate this explanatory power let us discuss the question of the need of knowledge justification: Why do we need at all to justify knowledge? From the rational theory of intuition outlined already, it follows that we must formulate in words and rationalize our concepts or theories before communicating them to others. Thus, the classical discourse of Heidegger (1957) about seven possible meanings of the words *nihil est sine ratione* can be supplemented by another meaning: An intuitive, preverbal judgment must be rationalized

---

* The word rationalization is used here in a neutral sense, without necessarily implying self-justification or advertisement, though they are often actually included. Rationalization is similar to knowledge justification, although justification is a broader and more objective, neutral concept.

when formulated and hence requires a ratio. Next comes an epistemological problem. If language was used as a tool of civilization evolution, individual thinkers were prompted to present their theories to the group, even to beautify and defend their theories—consistently with the Kuhnian concept of a *paradigm*. Such creative individuals might have been rewarded evolutionary, since eloquence might be considered as a positive aspect of mating selection. However, the evolutionary interest of the group that used the knowledge to enhance survival capabilities was the opposite: Personal theories that were too flowery must have been considered suspicious; Popperian *falsification* was necessary. Thus, Popperian falsification and Kuhnian paradigm are not contradictory; they represent different perspectives: that of a group and that of an individual; both were needed evolutionarily.

The rational theory of intuition outlined here allows also various other practical conclusions that might serve for its further falsification. For example, when it comes to personal intuition, this theory implies that our best ideas for intuitive decisions might come after a long sleep, before we fill our mind with the troubles of everyday life, hence, a simple rule we can call *alarm clock method*: Put on your alarm clock 10 minutes before normal time of waking, and immediately after waking ask yourself, Do I already know the solution to my most difficult problem? This simple experiment might serve as an empirical or falsification test of the rational theory of evolution.

6.5 Spirals of Knowledge Creation and Justification

If most new ideas are created intuitively, then most knowledge creation processes include interaction between intuitive and rational phases, as indicated by the outline of intuitive decision process presented already. While using the concept *tacit knowing* introduced by Polanyi (1966), Nonaka and Takeuchi (1995) introduced a spiral-like model called the SECI (Socialization-Externalization-Combination-Internalization) spiral (see Figure 6.6 on p. 126) of organizational knowledge creation, including transitions between tacit and explicit knowledge as well as individual and group knowledge.

This has motivated Wierzbicki and Nakamori (2006) to analyze the concept of a *creative space* (Figure 6.2), understood as a network-like model of diverse nodes between which various knowledge creation processes can occur, most of them having spiral-like character.

The creative space has three levels (i.e., individual, group, and the entire intellectual heritage of humanity) and three columns (i.e., emotional, intuitive, and rational). The creative space can have also other dimensions and nodes beside those shown in Figure 6.2, but this figure shows the possibility of diverse, mostly spiral-like processes between the nodes of this space. Wierzbicki and Nakamori (2006, 2007a) showed that there are many spirals

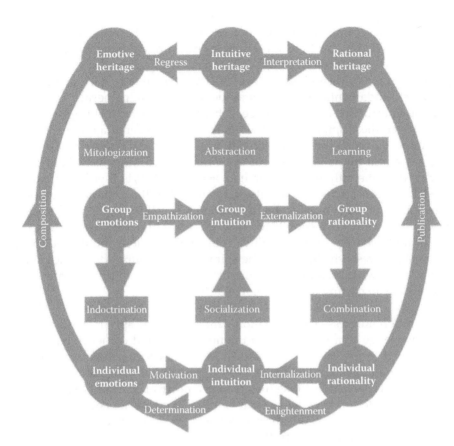

FIGURE 6.2
Basic dimensions of creative space.

of knowledge creation. Some of them are of an organizational character, typical of market innovations and practice-oriented organizations; some are of a normal academic character, typical of universities and research-oriented organizations.

Normal academic research actually combines three spirals:

1. Hermeneutics (gathering scientific information and knowledge from literature, the web, and other sources, interpreting, and reflecting upon these materials), which we call the EAIR (Enlightenment-Analysis-Immersion-Reflection) spiral.

2. Debate (group discussions about ongoing research), called the EDIS (Enlightenment-Debate-Immersion-Selection) spiral.

3. Experiment (testing ideas and hypotheses by experimental research), called the EEIS (Enlightenment-Experiment-Interpretation-Selection) spiral.

These three spirals do not exhaustively describe all that happens in academic knowledge creation; for example, planning research or roadmapping is also important and might be described in relation to the *i*-System (Nakamori, 2000; Ma and Nakamori, 2004). On the other hand, they describe the most fundamental elements of academic research: gathering and interpreting information and knowledge, debating, and experimenting.

However, these spirals are individually oriented. Even if a university or a laboratory supports them, the motivation and the actual research for preparing a doctoral thesis is mostly an individual effort. Moreover, these three spirals describe only what researchers actually do. It is thus a descriptive model; one can discuss the details of this model or the importance of separate spirals or their parts (called transitions), but the practice of academic research actually corresponds to these three spirals. Such models help in better understanding some intuitive transitions in these spirals and make it possible to test which parts of the spirals are well supported in academic practice and which require more support, but they do not produce any clear conclusions regarding how to organize research.

Moreover, there are several other creative spirals. One is the ARME (Abstraction–Regress–Mitologization–Empathization) spiral of revolutionary knowledge creation, visible in the upper left-hand corner of Figure 6.2 and related to the theory proposed in Motycka (1998), which we will not discuss here in detail since it is a macro-theory of knowledge creation (how knowledge is created in a long historical perspective). Instead, we focus here on micro-models of knowledge creation (how to create not necessarily revolutionary but also small advances of knowledge for the needs of today and tomorrow and how to justify them). But three other spirals are important for practical knowledge creation and for innovations, particularly in industry and other purpose-oriented organizations. These are the organizational creative spirals, motivated by purposes of a group and aimed at using the creative power of the group; here the individual's role is that of a member of the group, not of an individual researcher:

1. The widely known SECI spiral (Nonaka and Takeuchi, 1995).

2. The brainstorming DCCV (Divergence–Convergence–Crystallization–Verification) spiral (Kunifuji, Kawaji, Onabuta, Hirata, Sakamoto, and Kato, 2004), which is actually older than the SECI spiral but formulated only recently.

3. The objective-setting OPEC (Objectives–Process–Expansion–Closure) spiral (Gasson, 2004), the occidental counterpart of the SECI spiral (which is of Oriental origin).

Each of these spirals has a different role and can be applied for different purposes, and all have their strengths. Unfortunately, they cannot be easily combined, because they do not share the same elements. However, their combination among themselves and also with the spirals of academic knowledge creation is important for several reasons:

- Combining these spirals might strengthen academic knowledge creation, because it would increase the role of the group supporting the individual research.
- Combining these spirals also might strengthen industrial innovation and knowledge creation, because those processes always contain also some individual elements that should be explicitly accounted for.
- Combining these spirals might help improve cooperation between industry and academic institutions in producing innovations, because it could bridge the gap between the different ways of conducting research in academia and in industry.

With these purposes, the JAIST Nanatsudaki model was developed (Wierzbicki and Nakamori, 2007a)—a prescriptive or exemplar* model of the process of knowledge and technology creation. It consists of seven creative spirals; the metaphor *nanatsudaki* refers to water swirls in the seven waterfalls (nanatsudaki) on Asahidai hill, close to JAIST. The seven spirals include the three academic and the three organizational spirals mentioned, supplemented by a planning or roadmapping spiral based on the *i*-system. The model is built following the assumption that its applications will concern technology creation or material science development; thus, the application phase consists of experimental work. The order of the seven spirals reflects experience in managing scientific research; the Nanatsudaki model is intended to be a prescriptive tool, and the construction of tools is an art based on experience and intuition.

Thus, although the model could start with any constitutive spiral, managerial experience tells us that it is always good to specify objectives—even if only tentatively—at the beginning of a creative process. Therefore, the model starts with objective setting (thus using a part or all of the OPEC spiral) and ends with applications, or experimental work, here represented by the EEIS spiral. A diagram of the model, without showing the details of each spiral, is given in Figure 6.3.

After setting objectives, it is good to research and interpret existing knowledge related to the object of study—gather research materials, immerse them into our intuitive object perception, reflect on them—that is, perform all or a part of the hermeneutic EAIR spiral.

After hermeneutic reflection, it is good to create ideas using the power of the group involved in the research process. At least three types of processes can be used for this purpose. One is socialization—the starting transition of the SECI spiral. Another is brainstorming, or the related DCCV spiral.

---

* Serving as an example to follow, a normative or prescriptive model.

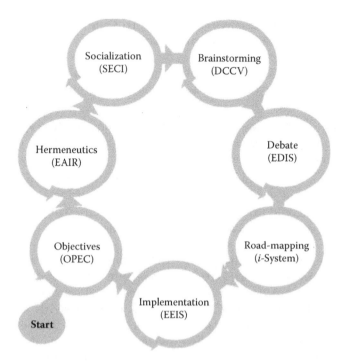

FIGURE 6.3
Diagram of JAIST Nanatsudaki model (septagram of creative spirals).

A classical academic method is debate, or the related EDIS spiral. In the Nanatsudaki model, they are used precisely in this order: Socialization can prepare for an effective brainstorming session, and a critical debate after brainstorming might also be helpful.

After a critical debate on research ideas, it is time for the detailed planning of the next stages of the research. Assuming that, on one hand, the experimental and final stages will be the most time-consuming and involve the most research effort but, on the other hand, after such intense preparation we know pretty much what we are going to do, this is the moment suitable for detailed planning or roadmapping.

After planning comes the actual implementation, here represented by the experimental EEIS spiral, possibly with many cyclic repetitions. The final closure of the entire process can be interpreted as a part of the beginning OPEC spiral, or even as a modified repetition of the entire seven-spiral process.

There are two possible interpretations of the previously depicted model. One is that each constitutive spiral of this septagram should be completed; that is, at least one cycle of the spiral should be realized. This is, however, a rather constraining interpretation, since creative spirals should start and end at any of their elements, without a prescribed number of cycles. Thus, we will describe the model while using a different interpretation: We might use any number of the elements (transitions) of the spirals, as necessary, sometimes without completing even one cycle, sometimes repeating more than one cycle.

The consecutive stages of the creative process represented by the model, together with their justification aspects, can thus be described in more detail in the following.

6.5.1 Objective Setting

Gasson (2004) rightly argues that the strength of Western (Occidental) industrial organization results from the good specification of the objectives of any activity. We assume here that the general objective is the best execution of a group research program, but more specific objectives should be set by the group, discussed by the members of the group, and used to motivate them in their joint work. The selection of the objectives is based on a vision and has an intuitive and emotional, tacit character; however, they must be communicated to the group and, thus, rationalized and justified. Justification of objectives relies on diverse arguments: reference to higher objectives, to logic and rationality.

We recall that Gasson's (2004) OPEC spiral consists of the following transitions: objectives (actual objective setting), process (delineating the steps to achieve the objectives), expansion (similar to enlightenment but not

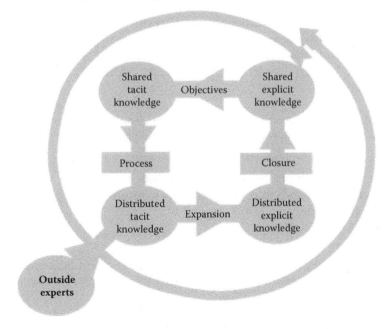

FIGURE 6.4
The OPEC spiral. (After Gasson, S., Proceedings of the 37th Hawaii International Conference on Systems Science, IEEE Computer Society Press, 2004.)

analyzed by Gasson in detail), and closure (summarizing and integrating the results achieved so far). The completion of a full OPEC cycle might not be needed at the beginning of the Nanatsudaki model. In its shortened realization, the transitions Objectives and an outline of Process might suffice, because later spirals of the Nanatsudaki model perform the functions of Expansion and Closure in more detail, although a full cycle might be tried if there is enough time for it. We stress that the objective setting and process outline in the beginning phase should be done in general and flexible terms, in the spirit of the Shinayakana systems approach (Sawaragi, Naito, and Nakamori, 1990). Such a general description should help all participants of the project, preparing them for individual efforts in the next stage. Detailed objective setting and process planning are postponed until the later road-mapping stage.

6.5.2   Hermeneutics

We use this humanistic concept (see, e.g., Gadamer, 1960) to describe the most basic activity for any research, be it in natural sciences or in technology—that of gathering relevant information and knowledge from outside sources, called here research materials, interpreting them, and reflecting on them. After setting the objectives and creating an outline of the working process, all members of the group should start this activity.

This does not mean that this activity is restricted only to Stage 2 of the Nanatsudaki Model; it should continue in parallel with all further steps, but it is essential that some research materials are gathered and reflected upon before Stage 3. Thus, at least one full cycle of the EAIR spiral should be completed here:

- Enlightenment corresponds here first to ideas for where and how to find research materials and later how to solve the overall problem.
- Analysis is a rational analysis of the research materials.
- Hermeneutic immersion means some time necessary to absorb the results of analysis into the individual's intuitive perception of the object of study.
- Reflection means intuitive preparation of the resulting new ideas.

The EAIR spiral is another representation of the so-called hermeneutic circle (Gadamer, 1960), assuming, however, that this circle is closed due to the power of intuition.*

---

* Hans Georg Gadamer (1960) assumes that closing the hermeneutic circle is due to transcendental powers of the human mind; we follow here the position of evolutionary naturalism and assume that the power of evolutionary developed intuition is strong enough for closing the circle.

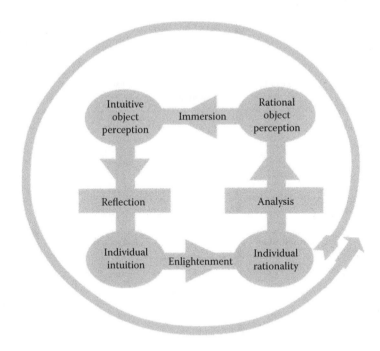

FIGURE 6.5
The hermeneutic EAIR spiral.

Further repetitions of the spiral should go on in parallel with other activities. Hermeneutics is the most individual research spiral, but its importance should be well understood, even in fully industrial group-based research. Hermeneutics is related to justification, but in a very special way: Our intuition compares holistically the gathered research materials with what we know fully.

6.5.3   Socialization

After hermeneutic research, all members of the group have some intuitive perception of the relevant problem of research; thus, they can start to use it in the SECI spiral. Nonaka and Takeuchi (1995) do not stress this, but they assume that the objectives of research are broadly outlined and that the intuitive perception—tacit knowledge—of individual group members already exists at the start of the SECI spiral:

Socialization in this spiral means sharing intuitive perceptions (in a typical Japanese way of sharing drinks after work).

Externalization means actually justification, rationalizing the intuitive knowledge of the group.

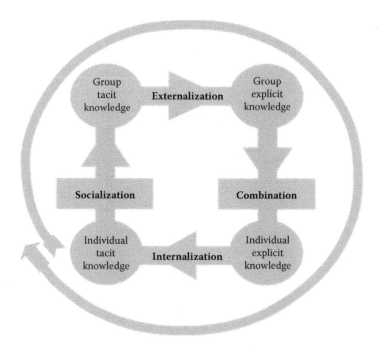

FIGURE 6.6
The SECI spiral. (After Nonaka, I. and Takeuchi, H. *The Knowledge-Creating Company: How Japanese Companies Create the Dynamics of Innovation*, Oxford University Press, 1995.)

> Combination means developing detailed plans and directives for individual group members, relying not only on this rationalized intuitive knowledge but also on all relevant external and humanity heritage knowledge.

> Internalization means increasing individual intuitive perception—tacit knowledge—while learning by doing.

However, again some spirals in further stages of the Nanatsudaki model perform the function of either externalization (as in brainstorming and debate) or combination (as in roadmapping) or even internalization (as in implementation) in more detail. Thus, the entire Nanatsudaki model can be interpreted as an enhanced SECI spiral, but in its separate part related to the SECI spiral it is sufficient to perform only the socialization. This is, however, a very important part, because without socialization the following brainstorming and debate might be not as effective.

6.5.4   Brainstorming

After socialization, the members of the group are well prepared for brainstorming. The full cycle of the DCCV spiral consists of the following:

- Divergence, also called divergent thinking transition, which is essential for generating as many and as wild ideas as possible.

- Convergence, or convergent thinking transition, which is helpful in organizing these ideas.

These two transitions are important for the entire Nanatsudaki model. The further transitions of *Crystallization*, or selection between organized ideas, and of *Verification*, or justification by comparison to human heritage knowledge or to results of experiments, are supported in more detail by the next spiral of debate and the final spiral of experiments.

However, the divergent thinking transition is extremely important for the success of the entire creative process: It mobilizes the full imaginative power of the group to generate new ideas. During this transition, the rules of divergent thinking—do not criticize, develop creatively even the wildest ideas—must be fully observed. On the other hand, the next convergent thinking transition requires switching back to a critical and synthetic attitude; since this never occurs easily, it is better to switch to another spiral for the crystallization of ideas.

6.5.5 Debate

If we separate this stage from brainstorming by at least one night, the members of the group have the opportunity to internalize the results of the former stage into their intuition; thus, they can better engage in debating these results.

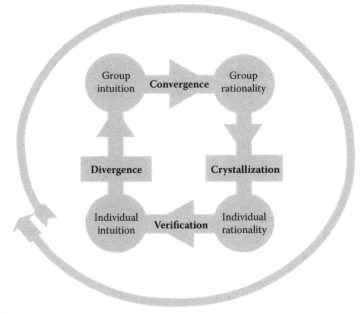

FIGURE 6.7
Brainstorming DCCV spiral. (After Kunifuji, S., Kawaji, T., Onabuta, T., Hirata, T., Sakamoto, R., Kato, N., Creativity Support Systems in JAIST, in proceedings of JAIST, 2004.)

Actually, the debate is a part of detailed realization of the difficult stages of combination from the SECI spiral or crystallization from the DCCV spiral: The list of ideas defined by group work must be made clear enough for every member of the group, and there is no better method for realizing that objective than by questioning and debating.

The EDIS spiral represents the interaction of explicit (rational) and tacit (emotional and intuitive) knowledge during a debate, as opposed to postmodernist approaches that underline only social aspects of discourse without realizing the role of individual (or even group) emotions and intuition:

- Enlightenment represents an individual generation of an idea, but might be replaced or supported by earlier socialization or brainstorming.

- Debate means actual debate of ideas, with diverse rules and traditions of discourse.

- Immersion means reflecting intuitively and emotionally during the debate on the points made by other participants.

- After the debate, each individual participant makes individual selection of most important conclusions of the debate.

As suggested in Wierzbicki and Nakamori (2006), if the EDIS spiral is performed separately, it is best to execute at least two cycles of it (the Principle

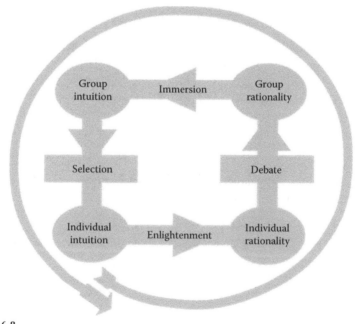

FIGURE 6.8
The EDIS spiral. (After Wierzbicki, A.P. and Nakamori, Y., *Creative Space: Models of Creative Processes for the Knowledge Civilization Age*, Springer-Verlag, 2006.)

of Double Debate) to fully mobilize group intuition. In the process of the Nanatsudaki model, however, the EDIS spiral uses the group intuition obtained by immersion of the results of brainstorming and in turn prepares group intuition for the next stage, roadmapping. Thus, it is sufficient to complete only one cycle of the EDIS spiral, starting with debate, and leaving some time—again, at least one night—for the internalization of results and intuitive selection of conclusions, preparing for the next stage of roadmapping. Again, it must be stressed that a well-organized debate is crucial: The members of the group have to switch their mind-sets, abandon the uncritical attitude of the former brainstorming stage, and start an open though constructive questioning of every assumption and of every doubt to achieve a better justification and a true crystallization of ideas.

6.5.6 Roadmapping

Roadmapping means including creative insights in detailed planning, in this case concerning further research activities. There are many forms of roadmaps, such as tables, graphs, and flowcharts. These are, however, just tools; the essence of a roadmapping process is a blueprint or normative model of the process that is being planned. Thus, the entire Nanatsudaki model might be a used as a blueprint for the roadmapping activity. Here we assume, however, that roadmapping is a part of the entire creative process and that its goal is to focus further research activities while using the results obtained so far, after the stages of objective setting, hermeneutics, socialization, brainstorming, and debate. Thus, there already are many partial results and ideas that must be focused to achieve the best final results.

Roadmapping with such a focused goal can be based on the *i*-system (Nakamori, 2000) or, rather, its representation as the I^5 spiral (Figure 6.9). All nodes in Figure 6.9 represent group knowledge, because roadmapping is assumed to be a group activity, but they correspond to group integrated, then rational, then intuitive, emotional, and again integrated knowledge. The transition Intelligence actually means summarizing all results of individual hermeneutic activities for use by the group, collecting all research material and partial results obtained so far. In planning future activities, this must also account for future hermeneutic and experimental activities, for implementation of the final research work, and for planning the final steps of the entire project and its expected results. However, such a plan of activities must be treated as only an outline, not a completed roadmap, because a mature roadmap can be obtained only after completing a full cycle of the I^5 spiral. The next transition, Involvement, means consultations—with social and economic experts, particularly the future users of the results of research project—about the outline of the plan and the expected results. After such consultations, the research group must reflect in the transition Imagination, thus immersing the consultation outcomes in their emotional knowledge and preparing the ground for a new integration. The Integration

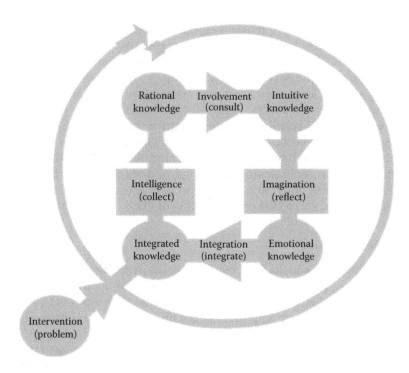

FIGURE 6.9
The I^5 spiral. (After Nakamori, Y., Knowledge Management System toward Sustainable Society, In Proceedings of the First International Symposium on Knowledge and System Sciences, 2000.)

transition occurs while working out a mature form of the roadmap for further research activities; thus, the integrated knowledge takes the form of a completed roadmap.

6.5.7   Implementation: Experimental Work

All the stages described until now could be used for a research project in any discipline—just as well for information sciences or social sciences and humanities. However, if the application of the Nanatsudaki model concerns material sciences or technology, then the actual implementation requires experimental work.

A spiral describing knowledge creation during individual experimental research consists (Figure 6.10) of the following:

- Enlightenment meaning the idea of an experiment
- Experiment performing the actual experimental work
- Interpretation of the experimental results reaching into the intuitive experimental experience of the researcher
- Selection of ideas to stimulate a new Enlightenment

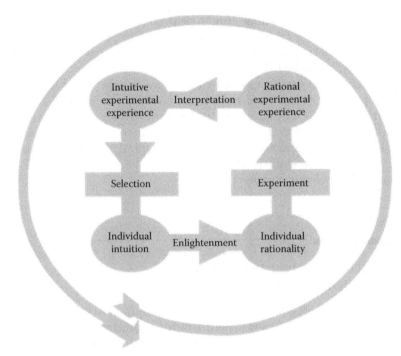

FIGURE 6.10
The EEIS spiral. . (After Wierzbicki, A.P. and Nakamori, Y., *Creative Space: Models of Creative Processes for the Knowledge Civilization Age*, Springer-Verlag, 2006.)

This cycle should be repeated as many times as needed and with such support as needed. The support might include interactive experiment planning; although the former roadmapping stage includes preliminary experiment planning, the results of current experiments and their interpretation always—at least in creative experimental work—imply changes in experiment planning. The support should also include experiment reporting, an extremely important aspect of experimental work in a group.

6.5.8 Closure: A Different Cycle of the Entire Process

A report of results obtained, a reflection on this summary of results, on their possible future implications and use, is always necessary upon completing a research project or an important stage of it. In a simpler case, this might be achieved just by repeating the first OPEC spiral of the process with a stress on the final transition of closure. However, for more complex cases, another cycle of the entire Nanatsudaki model process might be used, suitably modified, and shortened, if necessary, to fit the purpose of reporting or summarizing the results. For example, a new socialization stage might be used to informally exchange ideas about the importance and future applications of the results; brainstorming might be performed again, if some future applications deserve it; debate might help create the best summary and presentation of entire project; roadmapping and implementation might be not needed, but a review of the original roadmap, comparing it with actual developments, might be helpful in reporting.

The Nanatsudaki model has been tested in diverse ways; for example, through a survey of academic knowledge creation processes at a Japanese research university. One of the conclusions drawn from this survey is empirical support for the essential importance of the three spirals of normal academic knowledge creation—the debating EDIS spiral, the experimental EEIS spiral, and the hermeneutic EAIR spiral, as well as the roadmapping I^5 spiral of planning knowledge creation processes.

6.6   Conclusions: Justification in Knowledge Creation Processes

We see that knowledge justification plays a fundamental role in knowledge creation processes: even if new ideas are mostly intuitive, we must test, rationalize, and justify them in diverse ways if only to convince other people about their validity. Since there is no absolute certainty, there is also no absolute justification, and all search of (mostly Western) philosophy for an absolute fundament for knowledge was doomed to fail. Justification of knowledge plays, however, a very important role in maintaining the human intellectual heritage and organizing and evaluating all emotional, intuitive, and rational knowledge amassed by humanity as a public resource.

We use diverse civilization tools when performing knowledge justification: for example, diverse types of logic (we already stressed that the type of logic must be selected as an adequate tool for a given field of applications); debate and discourse; hermeneutic reflection; experimental testing whenever appropriate, especially in technology development that requires the design of critical tests; paradigmatic justification with exemplar theories; and falsification. All these tools are necessary, because human knowledge creation is a positive feedback phenomenon with avalanche-like processes; we must be sure that we pass to future generations only such knowledge that has positive significance in the evolution of civilization.

7

Knowledge Construction*

Yoshiteru Nakamori

Japan Advanced Institute of Science and Technology

CONTENTS

This chapter considers the problem of knowledge integration and proposes a theory of knowledge construction systems, which consists of three fundamental parts: a knowledge construction system, a structure–agency–action

---

* The contents of this chapter are part of a paper in Nakamori, Y., Wierzbicki, A. P., and Zhu, Z., A theory of knowledge construction systems, *Systems Research and Behavioral Science*, 28:15–39, 2011.

paradigm, and evolutionary constructive objectivism. The first is a model of collecting and synthesizing knowledge, the second relates to necessary abilities of actors when collecting knowledge in individual domains, and the third comprises a set of principles to justify collected and synthesized knowledge. The chapter starts with a brief introduction of a basic systems approach called informed systems thinking, followed by a summary of the theory of knowledge construction systems. The chapter then explains its three fundamental parts with an explanation of characters of the theory.

7.1 Introduction

The main principle of the theory of organizational knowledge creation proposed by Nonaka (Nonaka, 1991, 1994; Nonaka and Takeuchi, 1995) is that new knowledge is created by the interaction of explicit and tacit knowledge. Tacit knowledge refers, in the field of knowledge management, to knowledge known by an individual, which is difficult to communicate to others because it includes emotions and intuition. Therefore, socialization and externalization are emphasized in Nonaka's theory to obtain group explicit knowledge from individual tacit knowledge via group tacit knowledge; the last is shared mental models and technical skills.

Some people do not believe that knowledge can be managed. For instance, Wilson (2002) argues that knowledge management appears to be very much equated with information management, and some people assume wrongly that tacit knowledge can be made explicit. Nevertheless, Nonaka's theory is revolutionary because it stresses steps leading to knowledge increase surely, based on the collaboration of a group in knowledge creation and on the rational use of tacit knowledge, which includes emotions and intuition.

Knowledge management, as we use the term, was first introduced by computer technology firms in early 1980s as a computer software technology. In the early 1990s, this term was adopted by management science and became a management discipline. This has led to two distinct views of how to interpret this term:

- As management of information relevant for knowledge-intensive activities, with emphasis on, for example, information technology and knowledge engineering
- As management of people in knowledge-related processes, with emphasis on organizational theory, learning, types of knowledge, and knowledge creation processes

These two views listed incompletely describe what knowledge management is; there is a third view:

- As management of human resources in knowledge civilization era, concentrating on knowledge workers, their education and qualities, with a proper understanding of technologists and technology.

As a systems scientist, the author wishes to cover these three views in the theory. In addition to creating new knowledge by managing tacit knowledge (i.e., managing people), this chapter's concern is to develop a methodology for integrating and synthesizing distributed knowledge (which is implicit for actors prior to analysis) and for nurturing knowledge synthesizers or coordinators. From this point of view, instead of using the term *knowledge creation* or *knowledge management*, this chapter uses the term *knowledge construction*.

Another important concept in Nonaka's theory is *ba*, which is a Japanese word meaning place. Nonaka uses it as *creative environment*; actually Nonaka (Nonaka and Konno, 1998; Nonaka, Toyama, and Konno, 2000) used ba to refer to the dynamic context which is shared and redefined in the knowledge creation process. Ba does not refer just to a physical space but includes virtual spaces based on the Internet, for instance, and also mental spaces that involve sharing experiences and ideas. They stated that knowledge is not something that can exist independently; it can exist only in a form embedded in ba, which acts as a context that is constantly shared by people.

Similar ideas exist in systems theory: For instance, Churchman (1970) states that all knowledge is dependent on boundary judgments. This chapter follows this idea in such a way that the theory chooses three important dimensions from the high-dimensional creative space (Wierzbicki and Nakamori, 2006) and requires actors to work well in each dimension in collecting and organizing distributed, tacit knowledge. These are intelligence (scientific dimension), involvement (social dimension), and imagination (creative dimension). When the theory is interpreted from a viewpoint of sociology, the creative space is considered as a social structure that constrains and enables human action and consists of a scientific-actual front, a social-relational front, and a cognitive-mental front corresponding, respective to the three dimensions.

The theory introduces two more dimensions—intervention and integration—which correspond to social action and knowledge from the sociological point of view. This chapter follows the definition of systemic intervention in Midgley (2000, 2004) that systemic intervention is purposeful action by an agent to create change in relation to reflection upon boundaries. Actors collect knowledge on all three structural dimensions or fronts and synthesize distributed knowledge to construct new knowledge. In this sense, the dimensions intervention and integration correspond to Midgley's systemic intervention. As Wang Yang-Ming, the 14th-century Confucianist, stated, knowledge and action are one, for purpose, and with consequences (Zhu, 2000).

The theory to be presented in this chapter aims at integrating systematic approach and systemic thinking; the former is mainly used in the dimensions intelligence, involvement, and imagination, and the latter is required in the dimensions intervention and integration. Leading systems thinkers today often emphasize holistic thinking (Jackson, 2003; Mulej, 2007), or meta-synthesis (Gu and Tang, 2005). They recommend and require *systems thinking* for a holistic understanding of the emergent characteristic of a complex system and for creating a new systemic knowledge about a difficult problem confronted. The theory aims at synthesizing objective knowledge and subjective knowledge, which inevitably requires intuitive, holistic integration.

With a similar idea, Wierzbicki, Zhu, and Nakamori (2006) proposed an informed, creative systemic approach, named informed systems thinking, which should serve as the basic tool of knowledge integration and support creativity. This systems thinking emphasizes three basic principles: (1) the principle of cultural sovereignty, (2) the principle of informed responsibility, and (3) the principle of systemic integration. If the first is a thesis, then the second is an antithesis and the third is a synthesis.

The problem here is how are we to perform systemic integration in the context of knowledge synthesis? One of the answers to this is the theory of knowledge construction systems, which consists of three fundamental parts: (1) a knowledge construction system (Nakamori, 2000, 2003); (2) a structure–agency–action paradigm (Nakamori and Zhu, 2004); and (3) evolutionary constructive objectivism (Wierzbicki and Nakamori, 2007b). The main characteristics of this theory are fusion of the purposiveness paradigm and purposefulness paradigm, interaction of explicit knowledge and tacit knowledge, and involvement of knowledge coordinators.

The rest of this chapter is organized as follows:

1. A systems approach is introduced briefly, which is called informed systems thinking. Then a summary of the theory of knowledge construction systems is given.

2. The main model for knowledge synthesis, called *i*-System, is introduced, with a special emphasis on the types of integration: specialized, interdisciplinary, and intercultural.

3. A sociological interpretation of the *i*-System is presented, which refers to the ability of actors in collecting and synthesizing knowledge. The universality of the *i*-System is also discussed.

4. A new episteme to justify collected and synthesized knowledge is explained, which is important in evaluating actions in collecting knowledge as well as knowledge synthesized or constructed.

5. A new systems theory for knowledge construction is presented, which is based on the aforementioned three factors: system, agency, and episteme.

6. Concluding remarks are given that emphasize the importance of knowledge science to nurture knowledge coordinators.

7.2 Summary of the Theory

Wierzbicki et al. (2006) proposed redefining systems science as the discipline concerned with methods for the intercultural and interdisciplinary integration of knowledge, including soft intersubjective and hard objective approaches, open and informed attitudes:

- Intercultural means an explicit accounting for and analysis of national, regional, even disciplinary cultures, trying to overcome the incommensurability of cultural perspectives by explicit debate of the different concepts and metaphors used by diverse cultures.
- Interdisciplinary approach has been a defining feature of systems science since Comte (1844) but has been gradually lost in the division between soft and hard approaches.
- Open and informed mean pluralist:
  - Not excluding by design any cultural or disciplinary perspectives, as stressed by soft systems approaches (Flood and Jackson, 1991; Jackson and Keys, 1984; Linstone, 1984).
  - Not excluding any perspectives due to ignorance or disciplinary paradigmatic belief, as stressed by hard systems approaches.

A basic novel understanding related to this thinking is the essential extension of the skeleton of science (Boulding, 1956). Wierzbicki et al. (2006) named this kind of thinking informed systems thinking, which consists of three principles (Figure 7.1):

1. The principle of cultural sovereignty: We can treat all separate levels of systemic complexity as independent cultures and can generalize from basic cultural anthropology: No culture shall be judged by using concepts from a different culture.

2. The principle of informed responsibility: No culture is justified in creating a cultural separation of its own area; it is the responsibility of each culture to inform other cultures about its own development and to be informed about development of other cultures.

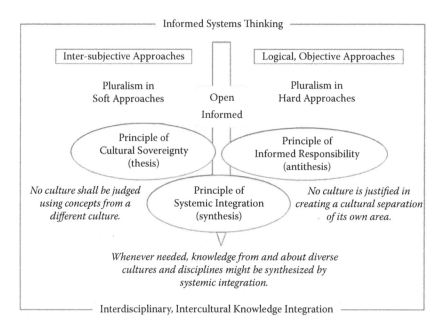

FIGURE 7.1
Informed systems thinking.

3. The principle of systemic integration: Whenever needed, knowledge from and about diverse cultures and disciplines may be synthesized by systemic integration, be they soft or hard, without prior prejudice against any of them.

It is, however, quite difficult to execute the principle of systemic integration unless we have theories or methods for knowledge construction. A summary of the theory of knowledge construction systems is now given, which consists of three fundamental parts:

1. The knowledge construction system: A basic system to collect and synthesize a variety of knowledge, called the *i*-System, which itself is a systems methodology (Nakamori, 2000, 2003).

2. The structure–agency–action paradigm: A sociological interpretation of the *i*-System to emphasize the necessary abilities of actors when collecting and synthesizing knowledge (Nakamori and Zhu, 2004).

3. The evolutionary constructive objectivism: A new episteme to create knowledge and justify collected and synthesized knowledge (Wierzbicki and Nakamori, 2007b).

The main characteristics of this theory are as follows:

- Fusion of the purposiveness paradigm and purposefulness paradigm
- Interaction of explicit knowledge and tacit knowledge
- Involvement of knowledge coordinators

The detail explanation of these characteristics will be given later. A brief summary is given next (see also Figure 7.2).

With the *i*-System, we always start by searching for and defining the problem according to the purposefulness paradigm. Since the *i*-System is a spiral-type knowledge construction model, in the second cycle we use the *i*-System to find solutions according to the purposiveness paradigm. However, it is almost always the case that when we find an approximate solution, we face new problems.

An important idea of Nonaka and Takeuchi (1995) is that new knowledge can be obtained by the interaction between the explicit and the tacit knowledge. The use of the *i*-System means that we must inevitably deal with objective knowledge such as scientific theories, available technologies, and socioeconomic trends as well as subjective knowledge such as experience, technical skills, hidden assumptions, and paradigms.

The theory requires people who accomplish the knowledge synthesis. Such persons need to have the abilities of knowledge workers and innovators in wide-ranging areas. However, they cannot achieve satisfactory results

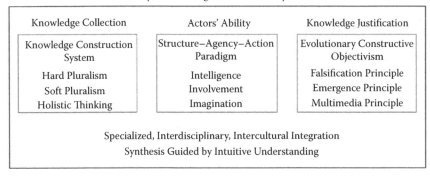

FIGURE 7.2
Theory of knowledge construction systems.

unless they also possess the ability to coordinate the opinions and values of diverse people. An educational system should be established to train human resources who will promote knowledge synthesis in a systemic manner.

7.3　Knowledge Construction System

A knowledge construction system called the *i*-System, proposed by Nakamori (2000, 2003), is a procedural (but virtually systemic) approach to knowledge creation. The five ontological elements or subsystems of the *i*-System are intervention (the will to solve problems), intelligence (existing scientific knowledge), involvement (social motivation), imagination (other aspects of creativity), and integration (systemic knowledge), and they might correspond actually to five diverse dimensions of creative space.

These five elements were originally interpreted as nodes, as illustrated in Figure 7.3. Because the *i*-System is intended as a synthesis of systemic approaches, integration is, in a sense, its final dimension (in Figure 7.3 all arrows converge to Integration interpreted as a node; links without arrows denote the possibility of impact in both directions). The beginning node is intervention, where problems or issues perceived by the individual or the

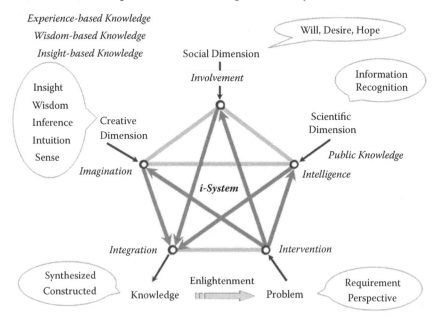

FIGURE 7.3
The *i*-System (from a systems scientific viewpoint).

group motivate their further inquiry and the entire creative process. The node intelligence corresponds to various types of knowledge; the node involvement represents social aspects; and the creative aspects are represented mostly in the node imagination.

7.3.1 Intelligence and Involvement

Observe that the node intelligence, together with all existing scientific knowledge, corresponds roughly to the basic epistemological dimension (with three levels: emotive knowledge, intuitive knowledge, and rational knowledge) of creative space. The node Involvement stresses the social motivation and corresponds roughly to the basic social dimension (with three levels: individual, group, and human heritage) of creative space.

When analyzing these dimensions Wierzbicki and Nakamori (2006) found that binary logic is inadequate, and even rough, three-valued logic barely sufficient for a detailed analysis. For example, it is necessary to distinguish not only between knowledge at the levels of the individual, the group, and human heritage but also motivation related to the interests of the individual, the group, and humanity. While an organization operating in the commercial market rightly stresses the interests of the group of people employed by it (or of its shareholders), educational research activity at universities might be best promoted when stressing the individual interests of students and young researchers; on the other hand, the interests of humanity must be protected when facing the prospect of privatization of basic knowledge (Figure 7.4).

7.3.2 Imagination

Other nodes in the *i*-System indicate the need to consider other dimensions of creative space, and additional dimensions result in additional complexity. The node imagination seems to be an essential element of only individual intuition, but it could include intersubjective emotions and intuition. All creative processes can be related to three levels of imagination: routine, diversity, and fantasy (Figure 7.4).

We use imagination in diverse degrees, depending on the character of a creative process. The lowest level is routine, which involves imagination, but in a standard, well-trained fashion. We are able to use imagination more strongly to involve an element of diversity, but we must be motivated to do this through, for example, professional pride, pure curiosity, or monetary rewards. Finally, we have also the highest level of imagination, which might be called fantasy. The 20th-century tradition of not speaking about metaphysics (started by Wittgenstein, 1922) relegated fantasy to the arts and the emotions. However, fantasy is an essential element of any highly creative process, including the construction of technological devices and systems.

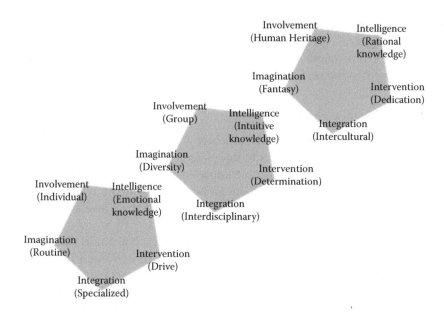

FIGURE 7.4
Three levels of five dimensions.

7.3.3   Intervention

The node Intervention is difficult to consider separately from the concepts of unity of mind and body and unity of humankind and nature in Oriental philosophy and culture: The will to do something is not considered as an independent phenomenon; it is simply a part of being, and being should be such as not to destroy the unity of humankind and nature. In a culture seeking consensus and harmony, such an explanation and such principles are sufficient for. Western cultures pay more attention to the problems related to human intervention and will. The concept of will, of freedom to act and intervene, has been for many centuries and still remains one of the central ideas of Western culture.

Concerning any creative activity, it is clear that the role of motivation, of the will to create new ideas, objects of art, or technological devices, is a central condition of success. Without drive, determination, and dedication, no creative process will be completed. By drive we understand here the basic fact that creativity is one of the most fundamental components of self-realization of humankind. Determination is the concentrated Nietzschean will to overcome obstacles in realizing the creative process. Dedication is a conviction that completing a creative process is right in terms of Kantian transcendental moral law.

7.3.4 Integration

Integration in the original *i*-System is a node intended to represent the final stage, the systemic synthesis of the creative process. Thus, in this stage we should use all systemic knowledge; application of systemic concepts to newly created knowledge is certainly the only explicit, rational knowledge tool that can be used to achieve integration. Thus, any teaching of creative abilities must include a strong component of systems science.

The apparently simplest is specialized integration, in which the task consists of integrating several elements of knowledge in some specialized field. But even this task can be very difficult as, for example, the task of integrating knowledge about the diverse functions of contemporary computer networks. The task becomes more complex when its character is interdisciplinary, as in the case of the analysis of environmental policy models. However, the contemporary trends of globalization result today in new, even more complex challenges related to intercultural integration, as in the case of integration of diverse theories of knowledge and technology creation. In fact, the intercultural Integration of knowledge might be considered a defining feature of a new interpretation of systems science.

Examples of three levels of integration follow:

1. Specialized integration: This example relates to the specialized knowledge integration process in a project for the development of translucent porcelain in the traditional industry in Japan. Actually Yamashita and Nakamori (2007) collected the following knowledge, created in recent technology development projects in that industry:

   a. Intervention: motivation (objective, mission, goal), external pressure (needs, requests), problem setting (subject, direction)

   b. Intelligence: research contents (methods, tools), research facilities, existing research (scientific knowledge, literature)

   c. Involvement: budget, collaboration (organizations, enterprises, persons), industrial conditions, social and cultural background (socioeconomic condition, fashion)

   d. Imagination: hint and idea (enlightenment), hidden story (trouble, failure), mind (ideal, interest, enthusiasm, change of heart)

   e. Integration: research results (contents, results, discovery), understanding (success or failure, new problems), evaluation (self-judgment, external evaluation), commodification (production, sale, patent), new research plans (for the next stage of the project)

2. Interdisciplinary integration: With a target of developing a fresh food management system, Ryoke, Yamashita, Hori, and Nakamori (2007) tried to integrate both hard systematic approach and soft systemic approach.

    a. Intervention: To deal with a demand prediction problem, a new approach was necessary to integrate the system engineering approach and the knowledge management approach. Ryoke et al. (2007) decided to collect knowledge about facts, social relations, and personal recognition in the dimensions of intelligence, involvement, and imagination.

    b. Intelligence: They constructed a mathematical demand prediction model based on past sales data, using, for example, data-mining techniques and clustering analysis, and developed a system for risk management to cope with waste loss as well as chance loss.

    c. Involvement: They collected and analyzed consumers' opinions, by a web-based questionnaire, to investigate important factors that affect purchasing decisions, which cannot be found from point-of-sale data or in managers' opinions.

    d. Imagination: From managers, they collected managerial knowledge including factors regarding decisions on kinds and amounts of goods and decisions regarding advertising promotions, taking into account special circumstances.

    e. Integration: They developed a management system consisting of a prediction subsystem, a risk analysis subsystem, and a managerial subsystem. However, the final decision should be made by a competent manager, who has experience and educated intuition, based on the outputs from the prediction and risk analysis system.

3. Intercultural integration: When establishing a plan for regional revitalization, taking into account, for example, environment, health care, and biomass, we have to consult authorities such as scientists, politicians, and economists as well as civil servants, and, most importantly, local residents. This requires interdisciplinary and intercultural integration of knowledge:

    a. Intervention: Let us consider the promotion of a biomass town* plan. Suppose that the problem is to find reasons for slow progress in establishing a biomass town.

    b. Intelligence: Investigate the existing scientific knowledge and the obstacles to promoting the biomass town plan, by interviewing researchers and civil servants.

    c. Involvement: Investigate the conception of people who already cooperate with this plan, asking them about the results so far and their evaluation of results.

---

* A biomass town refers to an area in which a proper profitable use of biomass is or will be executed, by constructing an overall profitable use system that connects generation of biomass with its effective use, under the wide cooperation of parties concerned.

    d. Imagination: Investigate consciousness of citizens about environmental problems, asking them what they know about the biomass town plan, how they learned about it, whether they are willing to cooperate with the plan, and why or why not.

    e. Integration: Assembling knowledge from the first three subsystems, summarize the problems in promotion of the biomass town plan.

7.3.5 Summary of the *i*-System

In summary, the knowledge construction system called the *i*-System is composed of five elements (dimensions, nodes, or subsystems):

1. Intervention: Taking action on a problem situation that has not been dealt with before. First we ask what kind of knowledge is necessary to solve the new problem? Then the following three subsystems are called on to collect that knowledge.

2. Intelligence: Enhancing our capability to understand and learn things. The necessary data and information are collected and scientifically analyzed, and then a model is built to achieve simulation and optimization.

3. Involvement: Heightening the interest and passion of ourselves and other people. Sponsoring conferences and collecting people's opinions using techniques like interview surveys.

4. Imagination: Creating our own ideas on new or existing things. Complex phenomena are simulated based on partial information by exploiting information technology.

5. Integration: Integrating heterogeneous types of knowledge so that they are tightly related. Validating the reliability and correctness of the output from the previous three subsystems.

The *i*-System is a systems methodology, with features according to Checkland's (1981) definition of a system: A system is characterized by hierarchy and emergence:

- Hierarchy: We can interpret the previous five elements variously—either as nodes or dimensions of creative space or subsystems. In the last interpretation, while the first and fifth subsystems are, in a sense, autonomous, the second, third, and fourth are dependent on others; it is generally difficult for them to complete their missions themselves, and thus we can introduce a lower level system with similar structure to the overall system. For instance, if we consider sustainable development, the role of subsystem intelligence might be prediction. However, this task cannot be completed by scientific knowledge only. This subsystem asks the lower system to collect data, to consider model structure, and to develop a mathematical model, which are the roles of involvement, imagination, and intelligence of the lower system.

- Emergence: Even if the *i*-System stresses that the creative process begins in the subsystem intervention and ends in the subsystem integration, it gives no prescription how to move between these subsystems. There is no algorithmic recipe for how to move between these ontological nodes or dimensions: all transitions are equally advisable, according to individual needs. This implicitly means that the *i*-System requires knowledge coordinators within the system; we have to refer to the abilities or agencies of coordinators that work in the previous three dimensions—intelligence, imagination, and involvement. Emergence (in a sense of knowledge synthesis or creation) can occur in the brains of actors or knowledge coordinators.

7.4 Structure–Agency–Action Paradigm

The structure–agency–action paradigm was adopted for understanding the *i*-System from a social science viewpoint (Nakamori and Zhu, 2004). The *i*-System can be interpreted as a structurationist model for knowledge management. Viewed through the *i*-System, knowledge is constructed by actors, who are constrained and enabled by structures that consist of scientific-actual, social-relational, and cognitive-mental fronts. These actors mobilize and realize the agency of themselves and of others, which can be differentiated as intelligence, involvement, and imagination clusters, and they engage in rational-inertial, a-rational-evaluative, and post-rational-projective actions in pursuing sectional interests. Note that here we identify the elements intelligence, involvement, and imagination with agencies of actors (Figure 7.5).

The following are working definitions of some key words that are essential to the present paradigm. These key words have quite different but deeply ingrained meanings in other disciplines, beyond contemporary social theories:

- Structure: the systemic contexts and their underlying mechanisms, which constrain and enable human action.
- Agency: the capability by which actors, who are socially embedded, reproduce and transform the world.
- Construction: the social process during which actors create, maintain, and transform the world (both the structure and actors themselves).

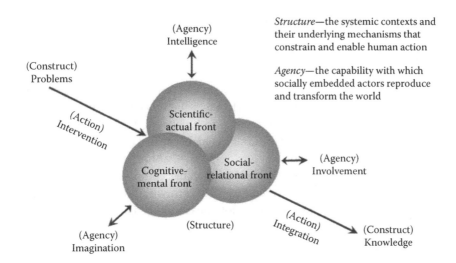

FIGURE 7.5
A sociological interpretation of the *i*-System.

The exploration in Nakamori and Zhu (2004) intended particularly to unpack the structure, agency, and action black boxes and to investigate the complexity, ambiguity, and emergent properties internal to each of them as well as the properties implicated in their inter-relationships. While structure complexity provides possibilities for innovation, agency complexity allows actors to exploit those possibilities in differing ways. Knowing (integrating or informing) and practice (intervening) are seen as complementing each other, and from them, knowledge emerges and is embodied, over time, back into structures and agency.

The exploration in Nakamori and Zhu (2004) drew mainly upon institutionalism (Scott, 1995), structuration theory (Bourdieu, 1985; Giddens, 1979, 1984, 1991; Jarzabkowski, 2004), critical realism (Archer, 1995; Bhaskar, 1989), and actor-network theory (Latour, 1987):

- Institutional theory proposes that the systemic environment consists of regulative, cognitive, and normative institutions that predispose coercive, mimetic, and normative isomorphic action; later also looks at institutional diversity, change, and entrepreneurship.

- Structuration theory is a social theory to overcome dualism, which contends that structure and agency simultaneously influence each other during social practice.

- Critical realism is a sociophilosophical theory, differing from structuration theory by emphasizing analytical dualism and temporal separability between structure and agency.

- Actor-network theory addresses the patterning of social practice, with particular focus on the evolution and institutionalization of technology.

With the *i*-System we conceive structure as consisting of scientific-actual, social-relational, and cognitive-mental fronts, which correspond to the scientific dimension, social dimension, and creative dimension, respectively. Here the word *front*, not dimension or domain, is used, because it conveys an indicative meaning in regard with constructivist view that, although scientific explanation is inherently partial, unstable, and contestable, continuously exploring scientific knowledge frontiers is a meaningful, worthwhile, and moral enterprise.

Table 7.1 gives a summary of terminologies explaining different words.

7.4.1 Agency Complexity

This section focuses on the agency complexity, which is directly related to the theory of knowledge construction systems. The *i*-System differentiates human agency into intelligence, involvement, and imagination clusters, so that agency can be understood in an organized way, not treated as a black box (Figure 7.6).

By intelligence we mean the intellectual faculty and capability of actors: experience, technical skill, functional expertise. The vocabulary related to intelligence addresses logic, rationality, objectivity, observation, monitoring, and reflexivity. The accumulation and application of intelligence are mission led and rational focused (Chia, 2004), discipline and paradigm bound, confined within the boundary of normal science (Kuhn, 1962), which leads

TABLE 7.1

A Summary of Terminologies

Nodes in the *i*-System	Systems-scientific viewpoint	Knowledge-scientific viewpoint	Social-scientific viewpoint
Intervention	a subsystem (input level)	a dimension (in creative space)	a social action
Intelligence	a subsystem (in the scientific dimension)	a dimension (epistemological dimension	an agency (in the scientific-actual front)
Involvement	a subsystem (in the social dimension)	a dimension (ontological dimension in creative space)	an agency (in the social-relational front)
Imagination	a subsystem (in the creative dimension)	a dimension (in creative space)	an agency (in the cognitive-mental front)
Integration	a subsystem (output level)	a dimension (in creative space)	a social action

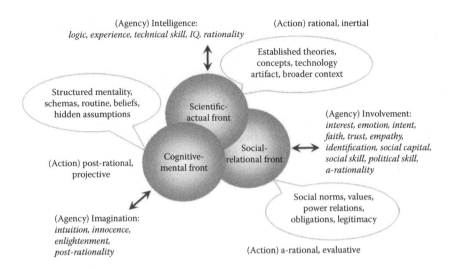

FIGURE 7.6
Structures, agencies, and actions.

to knowing the game and incremental, component improvement (Tushman and Anderson, 1986).

Seeing intelligence as inertial and paradigm bound though, the *i*-System does not regard intelligence as negative per se. Rather, to the *i*-System, intelligence is indispensable for creativity. As Polanyi (1958) stated, science is operated by the skill of the scientist, and it is through the exercise of this skill that he or she shapes scientific knowledge. Following Sewell (1992), we see the search for intelligence as a process of transposition: Actors apply and extend codified rules and procedures to a wide and not fully predictable range of unfamiliar cases outside the context in which they are initially learned. Intelligence becomes liability to innovation only when it blocks actors from seeing alternatives.

Involvement is the cluster in human agency that consists of interest, faith, emotion, and passion, which are intrinsically related to intentionality and habits of the heart (Bellah et al., 1985), as well as the social capital (Bourdieu, 1985), social skill, and political skill (Garud et al., 2002). As human agency, involvement can produce managerial and institutional effects, particularly in dealing with the social-relational front, in that it helps or hampers researchers' efforts to make the game.

In the imagination cluster we include intuition, innocence, ignorance, and enlightened skill, which lead to the vocabulary of feeling the game, playful, fun, chaotic, illogic, forgetting, upsetting. This brings us beyond the thoroughly knowledgeable (Archer, 1995) and overrationalized agents (Mestrovic, 1998) that are portrayed in Giddens's structuration theory (Giddens, 1979).We turn to the naturalist Taoism, the transcendental Zen Buddhism, and the pragmatic Confucianism. Zhuang Zi, the Taoist sage, famously proclaims that great knowledge is like a child's ignorance. He distinguishes three kinds of knowledge: prerationality (child's knowledge, or primary ignorance); rationality (adult's knowledge, i.e., great artifice, which denotes established theories, concepts, categories, normal science, and associated findings); and postrationality (absence of knowledge, or true knowledge, i.e., the knowledge of the True-man).

Note that even if the actors work well using their agencies, this does not guarantee the validity of the obtained knowledge. We need a theory of knowledge justification, which will be given later by the name evolutionary constructive objectivism.

7.4.2   Key Propositions

Nakamori and Zhu (2004) unpacked the structure, agency, and action black boxes, discussing their internal complexity as well as the implications of the relationships between them. For this, in addition to Western social theories they drew also from Taoism and Buddhism and ideas from the realist Cheng-Zhu and the idealist Lu-Wang schools of neo-Confucianism (see Zhu, 1998, 1999, 2000). The key propositions in Nakamori and Zhu (2004) are summarized as follows:

- Both knowledge-as-construct (the realist Confucianism) and knowing-in-practice (the idealist Confucianism) are indispensable for knowledge construction. Knowledge, stabilized in structure and agency at focal empirical moments, provides actors material, intellectual, as well as social capacities and contexts to conduct social action, because action transforms knowledge, for the better or the worse, which is embodied back into structure and agency, over time.

- Construction is meant to be practical, temporal, and relational. Knowledge is not created if creation means, as it does in popular knowledge creation models, well ordered, linearly progressive, interest free, politically neutral, and intellectually beyond dispute. Rather, knowledge is better seen as always and constantly ambiguous, contextual, provisional, contestable, negotiated, agreed upon, informing, constituting, and legitimating.

- The *i*-System brings the heart back into knowledge agendas rather than shying away from the heart or taking it for granted. While knowledge enhances material well-being and spiritual sophistication, at least for some on the globe, it also grants humans awesome power to do ugly things to Nature and among humans. Are knowledge, technology, and innovation necessarily good things? How and who to manage them for good, good for Nature and all, not just the few? These are, to the *i*-System, legitimate and relevant questions in knowledge management, which is not equivalent to knowledge commodification.

- Rooted in systems science, the *i*-System intends to be integrative in spirit. A system to us is a set of components connected such that properties emerging from them cannot all be found in components. Yin and yang never melt down into a synthesis, the loss of opposites means death. Hence, integration is about openness, tolerance, interdisciplinary, and intercultural, it is an interactive and reciprocal process of perspective making and taking (Boland and Tenkasi, 1995) and sharing and enriching, not of programming heterogeneity into homogeneity by the magic hand of system experts.

7.4.3 Universality of the *i*-System

The multifront, multicluster, multidimensional aspects of the *i*-System conceptions can be seen as rooted in Confucianism, a life philosophy of the Chinese and the Japanese which is modeled based on the eight wires in "Da Xue" (The Great Learning), a chapter in a 3,000-year-old classic, *Li Ji* (The Book of Rites). The eight wires have been subsequently categorized into three broad groups: (1) investigating things, extending knowledge; (2) being sincere, rectifying the mind, cultivating the self; and (3) regulating the family, governing the state, pacifying the world (Chan, 1963; Cheng, 1972; Linstone and Zhu, 2000; Zhu, 2000). Although mainly concerned with epistemology (how to know) and methodology (how to do) in social life and lacking sufficient concern with metaphysics, the Confucian teaching implies a latent view of reality: reality as a complex web of relations: relation with Nature, relation with mind, relation with humans (others). The *i*-System conceptions of structure, agency and action are to us therefore all informed by these chordal triad relations.

There are interesting affinities of the *i*-System's conceptual multiplicity with, beneath diverse and perhaps confusing terminologies, Giddens's (1979) facility, interpretive scheme and norm modalities; Habermas's (1972) three worlds and corresponding human interests and knowledge; Archer's (1995) structural and cultural conditions; Scott's (1995) regulative, cognitive, and normative pillars of institutions; Child's (1997) material, cognitive, and relational structures; Nahapiet and Ghoshal's (1998) structural, cognitive, and relational dimensions of social/intellectual capital; and Garud and Rappa's (1994) three basic definitions of technology—technology as objective artifacts, as subjective beliefs, and as legitimized normative evaluation routines.

This strengthens the belief that the *i*-System's sociological underpinning is, on one hand, localized and culturally bound, as manifested in its emphasis on ignorance, emotion, and dialectics in terms of oppositional complementarities rather than of the thesis-antithesis-synthesis grand order. But it is, on the other hand, universal, on the grounds that the *i*-System shares many similar concerns, values, and conceptual patterns, such as chordal triad conceptions, with its Western counterparts, which we see as being at odds with the clash of civilizations' thesis (Huntington, 1993, 1996).

7.5   Evolutionary Constructive Objectivism

There is a general agreement that we are living in times of an informational revolution, which is leading to a new era. Knowledge in this era plays an even more important role than just information; thus the new epoch might be called the knowledge civilization era. Among many changes, the most important one might be the changing episteme—the way of constructing and justifying knowledge, characteristic for a given era and culture (Foucault, 1972).

The destruction of the industrial episteme and the construction of a new one started with the relativism of Einstein, the indeterminism of Heisenberg, and with the concept of feedback and deterministic chaos, of order emerging out of chaos, complexity theories, and finally with the emergence principle. The destruction of the industrial era episteme resulted in divergent developments of the episteme of three cultural spheres: hard and natural sciences, technology, and social sciences with humanities:

Paradigmatism in hard and natural sciences (Kuhn, 1962): Theories should fit to observations or outcomes of empirical tests, but such theories that are consistent with the paradigm are welcome, while theories that contradict the paradigm are rejected, even if they would better fit observations or empirical outcomes.

Falsificationism in technology (Popper, 1934, 1972): Knowledge and theories evolve and the measure of their evolutionary fitness is the number of attempted falsification tests they have successfully passed.

Postmodern subjectivism in social sciences and humanities: Knowledge is constructed by people, thus subjective, and its justification occurs only through intersubjective discourse.

The episteme of knowledge civilization era is not formed yet, but it must include integration, a synthesis of the divergent episteme of these three cultural spheres, as well as a synthesis of different aspects of Oriental and Western episteme. The integration must be based upon a holistic understanding of human nature; here humanity is defined not only by language and communication but also by tool making, and by curiosity.

Evolutionary constructive objectivism can be considered as a possible episteme in the knowledge-based society, and it was adopted as one of the elements of the theory of knowledge construction systems. It was originally considered for testing knowledge creation theories (Wierzbicki and Nakamori, 2007b), consisting of three principles:

Evolutionary falsification principle: Hypotheses, theories, models, and tools develop evolutionarily, and the measure of their evolutionary fitness is the number of either attempted falsification tests that they have successfully passed or of critical discussion tests leading to an intersubjective agreement about their validity, which corresponds to the group tacit knowledge in Nonaka's theory of organizational knowledge creation.

Emergence principle: New properties of a system emerge with increased levels of complexity, and these properties are qualitatively different from and irreducible to the properties of its parts.

Multimedia principle: Language is just an approximate code to describe a much more complex reality; visual and preverbal information in general is much more powerful and relates to intuitive knowledge and reasoning. The future records of the intellectual heritage of humanity will have a multimedia character, thus stimulating creativity.

Although these principles were developed with the purpose of validating knowledge creation models such as the *i*-System, they are reused here to test knowledge obtained. Because it usually takes time to evaluate new knowledge, the idea here is to evaluate the models, methods or processes through which the new knowledge emerges (Figure 7.7).

Based on these three fundamental principles, a detailed description of an epistemological position of evolutionary constructive objectivism is given

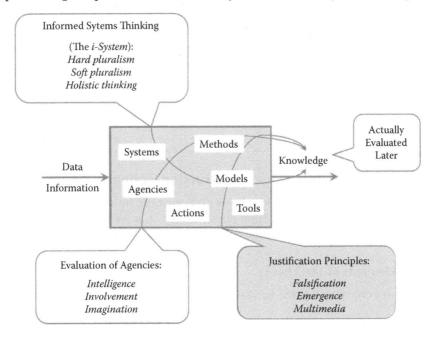

FIGURE 7.7
Justification of knowledge through evaluation of tools to acquire it.

following, which is closer in fact to the current episteme of technology than to that of hard sciences:

- The innate curiosity of people about other people and Nature results in their constructing hypotheses about reality, thus creating a structure and diverse models of the world. Until now, all such hypotheses turned out to be only approximations, but we learn evolutionarily about their validity by following the falsification principle.

- Since we perceive reality as more and more complex and thus devise concepts on higher and higher levels of complexity according to the emergence principle, we shall probably always work with approximate hypotheses.

- According to the multimedia principle, language is a simplified code used to describe a much more complex reality, while human senses (starting with vision) enable people to perceive more complex aspects of reality. This more comprehensive perception of reality is the basis of human intuition; for example, tool making is always based on intuition and a more comprehensive perception of reality than that provided by language.

- A prescriptive interpretation of objectivity is the falsification principle; when faced cognitively with increasing complexity, we apply the emergence principle. The sources of our cognitive power are related to the multimedia principle.

Figure 7.7 shows the concept of justification of knowledge through evaluation of, for example, models and tools to acquire that knowledge as well as through evaluation of attitudes and agencies of actors or analysts in collecting that knowledge.

7.6 Theory of Knowledge Construction Systems

In the context of knowledge synthesis and creation, how can we perform a systemic integration? This section summarizes an answer to this question, which is the theory of knowledge construction systems (Figure 7.8).

7.6.1 Elements of the Theory

The theory consists of three fundamental elements:

1. The knowledge construction system (the *i*-System)
2. The structure–agency–action paradigm
3. The evolutionary constructive objectivism

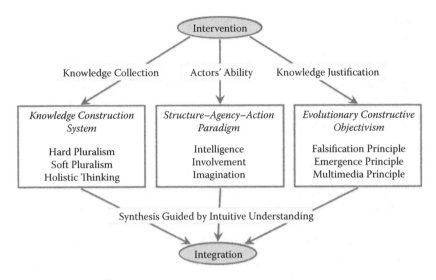

FIGURE 7.8
Systemic intervention for knowledge integration.

7.6.1.1 Knowledge Construction System

The *i*-System is regarded as a concrete methodology of informed systems thinking and is characterized as follows:

- Hard pluralism at intelligence (according to the principle of informed responsibility)
  - Try to examine a variety of methods and tools without a prior prejudice against them, based on a belief of disciplinary paradigm.
  - Try to treat not only rational knowledge but also intuitive knowledge, and further, emotional knowledge.
- Soft pluralism at involvement (according to the principle of cultural sovereignty)
  - Try to take into account any cultural, disciplinary standpoints.
  - Try to have a sense of proportion for the benefit of individual, group, and society.
- Holistic thinking at Imagination (use of experience-, insight-based knowledge, wisdom)
  - Try to imagine, simulate the future based on a variety of information.
  - Try to stimulate idea generation by brainstorming or information techniques.

However, the *i*-System does not clearly prepare any ready answer to the question: How can we perform a systemic knowledge integration? Instead, the *i*-System emphasizes:

- Repetition of intervention and integration for systemic intervention.
- Involvement of knowledge coordinators as elements of the system to achieve the principle of systemic integration.

7.6.1.2 Structure–Agency–Action Paradigm

In collecting knowledge the *i*-System requires actors to have the following agencies:

- Intelligence in the scientific dimension (scientific-actual front)
  - Capability of actors: experience, technical skill, functional disciplinary knowledge
  - Attitude of actors: logical, rational, objective
- Involvement in the social dimension (social-relational front)
  - Capability of actors: intellectual enthusiasm, faith, openness
  - Attitude of actors: empathetic, moral, a-rational
- Imagination in the creative dimension (cognitive-mental front)
  - Capability of actors: insight, judgment, curiosity
  - Attitude of actors: subjective, intuitive, post-rational

7.6.1.3 Evolutionary Constructive Objectivism

Collected, synthesized, or created knowledge should be justified by the following principles:

- Evolutionary falsification principle
  - Evolutionarily developed knowledge is tested by falsification in the broadest sense, including intersubjective falsification through critical discussions.
  - Descriptive theories are tested by critical experiments and prescriptive theories are tested by repetition of applications.
- Emergence principle
  - This fundamental principle is related to the emergence of new concepts and properties at higher levels of complexity.
  - When confronting a complex problem, do not hesitate to create a new concept.

- Multimedia principle
  - Pay attention to visual and preverbal information, which is much more powerful than words, and relates to intuitive knowledge and reasoning.
  - Pay attention to various aspect of information to enhance holistic understanding and complete synthesis.

7.6.2 Characteristics of the Theory

The main characteristics of this theory are as follows:

- Fusion of the purposiveness paradigm and purposefulness paradigm
- Interaction of explicit knowledge and tacit knowledge
- Involvement of knowledge coordinators

7.6.2.1 Fusion of Paradigms

With the *i*-System we always start with searching for and defining the problem following the purposefulness paradigm. Since the *i*-System is a spiral-type knowledge construction model, in the second cycle we use the *i*-System to find solutions following the purposiveness paradigm. However, it is almost always the case that just when we have found an approximate solution we face new problems.

By introducing a viewpoint of knowledge construction, the *i*-System enables us to have purposiveness and purposefulness paradigms simultaneously (Figure 7.9):

1. We start any problem solving with a desire to collect some knowledge. Let us denote this knowledge by A.
2. The first use of the *i*-System is to investigate what kinds of knowledge are actually available. Actors usually obtain integrated knowledge, which might consist of explicit intellectual assets, implicit or tacit knowledge among people, and knowledge that actors already have. Denote this integrated knowledge by B.
3. Almost always there is a difference between A and B. There is probably some knowledge that actors cannot obtain despite their best endeavor. This pursuit is a trade-off with limited time.
4. Actors have to create new knowledge C to fill in the gap between A and B. The *i*-System cannot have C in advance. The creation of C is the work of actors who are embedded in the *i*-System. If the creation of C is difficult, actors have to restart searching for it with the *i*-System.

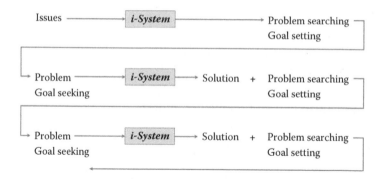

FIGURE 7.9
Fusion of the purposiveness and purposefulness paradigm.

7.6.2.2 Interaction of Explicit and Tacit Knowledge

Recall the idea of Nonaka and Takeuchi (1995) that the new knowledge can be obtained by the interaction between explicit knowledge and tacit knowledge. The use of the *i*-System means that we have to inevitably treat objective knowledge such as scientific theories, available technologies, and socioeconomic trends as well as subjective knowledge such as experience, technical skill, hidden assumptions, and paradigms, and most importantly we have to integrate them for a certain purpose (Figure 7.10).

7.6.2.3 Knowledge Coordinators

The theory requires people who accomplish the knowledge synthesis. Such persons need to have the abilities of knowledge workers and of innovators in wide-ranging areas. However, they cannot achieve satisfactory results

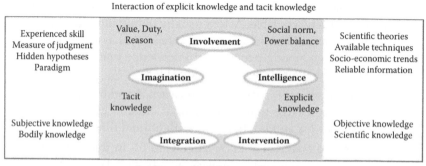

FIGURE 7.10
Interaction of explicit and tacit knowledge.

unless they possess the ability to coordinate the opinions of people and diverse knowledge. We should establish an education system to train human resources who will promote the knowledge synthesis in a systemic manner.

7.7 Concluding Remarks

This chapter introduced a theory of knowledge construction systems, which consists of three fundamental parts: the knowledge construction system, the structure–agency–action paradigm, and evolutionary constructive objectivism. The first part is a model of collecting and synthesizing knowledge; the second relates to necessary abilities when collecting knowledge in individual domains; and the third comprises a set of principles to justify collected and synthesized knowledge. One of the conclusions in this chapter is that we should nurture talented people, called the knowledge coordinators. How can we nurture such people? One of the answers is that we should establish knowledge science, educate young students by this discipline, and encourage learning by doing.

However, at the present stage, knowledge science is more a theme-oriented interdisciplinary academic field than a usual science. Its mission is to organize and process human-dependent information and to feed this information back to society with added value. The central guideline of knowledge science is the creation of new value called knowledge, which is the driving force of society. Because society's progress is underpinned by technology, knowledge science bears the duty to act as a coordinator or social and technological innovations.

To fulfill its mission, knowledge science should focus its research on observing and modeling the actual process of carrying out the mission as well as developing methods to carry out the mission. The methods can be developed mainly through the application of information technology/artistic methods (e.g., knowledge discovery methods, ways to support creation, knowledge engineering, cognitive science), the application of business science/organizational theories (e.g., practical uses of tacit knowledge, management of technology, innovation theory), and the application of mathematical science/systems theory (e.g., systems thinking, the emergence principle, epistemology). However, it will take some time to integrate the above fields and establish a new academic system. We should first attempt their integration in practical use (problem-solving projects), accumulate actual results, and then establish knowledge science from different disciplinary viewpoints.

References

Ackoff, R.L. 1994. Systems thinking and thinking systems. *Systems Dynamic Review* 10:175–188.

Applehans, W., Globe, A., and Laugero, G. 1999. *Managing knowledge: A practical web-based approach*. Reading, Mass: Addison-Wesley Professional.

Archer, M.S. 1995. *Realist social theory: The morphogenetic approach*. Cambridge, UK: University of Cambridge Press.

Assudani, R.H. 2005. Catching the chameleon: Understanding the elusive term "knowledge." *Journal of Knowledge Management* 9(2):31–44.

Augen, J. 2005. *Bioinformatics in the post-genomic era: Genome, transcriptome, proteome, and information-based medicine*. Boston, MA: Addison-Wesley.

Baeza-Yates, R., and Ribeiro-Neto, B. 1999. *Modern information retrieval*. Boston, MA: Addison-Wesley-Longman.

Baldi, P., and Brunak, S. 2001. *Bioinformatics: The machine learning approach*. Cambridge, MA: MIT Press.

Becerra, I., Gonzalez, A., and Sabherwal, R. 2004. *Knowledge management: Challenges, solutions, and technologies*. Upper Saddle River, NJ: Pearson Education, Inc.

Bellah, R.N., Madsen, R., Sullivan, M.M., Swidler, A., and Tipton, S.M., eds. 1985. *Habits of the heart*. Berkeley, CA: University of California Press.

Bergson, H. 1903. *Introduction à la métaphysique*. Paris: Suresnes. Translated by T. E. Hulme as *An introduction to metaphysics*. London: Macmillan, 1913.

Bhaskar, R. 1989. *The possibility of naturalism*. Brighton, UK: Harvester.

Bishop, C.M. 2006. *Pattern recognition and machine learning*. Berlin: Springer-Verlag.

Blei, D.M., Ng, A.Y., and Jordan, M.I. 2003. Latent dirichlet allocation. *Journal of Machine Learning Research* 3:993–1022.

Boland, R.J., and Tenkasi, R.V. 1995. Perspective making and perspective taking in communities of knowing. *Organisation Science* 6:350–372.

Boulding, K. 1956. General systems theory: The skeleton of science. *Management Science* 2:197–208.

Bourdieu, P. 1985. The forms of capital. In *Handbook of theory and research for the sociology of education*, ed. J. G. Richardson, 241–258. New York: Greenwood.

Braudel, F. 1979. *Civilisation matérielle, économie et capitalisme, XV–XVIII siècle*. Paris: Armand Colin.

Brin, S., and Page, L. 1998, April 14–18. The anatomy of a large-scale hypertextual Web search Eengine. In *Proceedings of the 7th international conference on World Wide Web* (WWW), 107–117. Brisbane, Australia.

Bunge, M. 1962. *Intuition and science*. New York: Prentice-Hall.

Chakrabarti, S. 2001. *Mining the Web: Discovering knowledge from hypertext data*. San Francisco: Morgan Kaufmann.

Chan, W. 1963. *A source book in Chinese philosophy*. Princeton, NJ: Princeton University Press.

Chapelle, O., Schölkopf, B., and Zien, A. 2006. *Semi-supervised learning*. Cambridge, MA: MIT Press.

Checkland, P.B. 1981. *Systems thinking, systems practice*. Chichester, UK: John Wiley and Sons.

Cheng, C.Y. 1972. Chinese philosophy: A characterization. In *Invitation to Chinese philosophy*, ed. A. Naess and A. Hannay, 141–165. Oslo: Universitetsforrlaget.

Chia, R. 2004. Strategy-as-practice: Reflections on the research agenda. *European Management Review* 1:29–34.

Child, J. 1997. Strategic choice in the analysis of action, structure, organisations and environment: Retrospect and prospect. *Organisation Studies* 18:43–76.

Churchman, C.W. 1970. Operations research as a profession. *Management Science* 17:37–53.

Cios, K.J., ed. 2000. *Medical data mining and knowledge discovery*. Heidelberg: Physica-Verlag.

Comte, A. 1844. *A general view of positivism*. London: Routledge. (Translation in 1865.)

Curtarolo, S., Morgan, D., Persson, K., Rodgers, J., and Ceder, G. 2003. Predicting crystal structures with data mining of quantum calculations. *Physical Review Letters* 91(13):135–503.

Curtarolo, S., Morgan, D., and Ceder, G. (2005). Accuracy of ab initio methods in predicting the crystal structures of metals: A review of 80 binary alloys, *Calphad: Computer Coupling of Phase Diagrams and Thermochemistry*, 29, 3, 163–211.

Dai, R., Yu, J.Y., and Gu, J.F. 2003, September 8–10. *A meta-synthetic approach for decision support system*. Presented at the 17th JISR-IIASA workshop on methodologies and tools for complex system modeling and integrated policy assessment. Austria.

Deerwester, S., Dumais, S.T., Furnas, G.W., Landauer, T.K., and Harshman, R. 1990. Indexing by latent semantic analysis. *Journal of American Society for Information Science* 41(6):391–407.

Dewey, J. 1910. *How we think*. Charleston, SC: BiblioLife, LLC.

Dreyfus, H., and Dreyfus, S. 1986. *Mind over machine: The role of human intuition and expertise in the era of computers*. New York: Free Press.

Einstein, A. 1905. Über die elektrodynamik von körpern in bewegung. *Annalen der Physik* 17:891–921.

Fayyad, U., Grinstein, G., and Wierse, A. 2001. *Information visualization in data mining and knowledge discovery*. San Francisco: Morgan Kaufmann.

Fayyad, U., Haussler, D., and Stolorz, P. 1996. Mining scientific data. *Communications of the ACM* 39(11):51–57.

Fayyad, U., Piatetsky-Shapiro, G., Smyth, P., and Uthurusamy, R., eds. 1996. *Advances in knowledge discovery and data mining*. Cambridge, MA: AAAI/MIT Press.

Flood, R.L., and Jackson, M.C. 1991. *Creative problem solving: Total systems intervention*. New York: John Wiley and Sons.

Fodor, J.A. 1994. *The elm and the expert: Mentalese and its semantic*. Cambridge, MA: MIT Press.

Foss, N. 2009. Alternative research strategies in the knowledge movement: From macro bias to micro-foundations and multi-level explanation. *European Management Review* 6:16–28.

Foucault, M. 1972. *The order of things: An archeology of human sciences*. New York: Routledge.

Franke, J., Nakhaeizadeh, G., and Renz, I. 2003. *Text mining: Theoretical aspects and applications*. Heidelberg: Physica-Verlag.

Freitas, A., Simon, A., and Lavington, H. 1998. *Mining very large databases with parallel processing*. Boston: Kluwer Academic Publishers.

Gadamer, H.G. 1960. *Warheit und methode. Grundzüge einer philosophishen Hermeneutik.* J.B.C. Mohr (Siebeck).

Garud, R., Jain, S., and Kumaraswamy, A. 2002. Institutional entrepreneurship in the sponsorship of common technological standards: The case of Sun Microsystems and Java. *Academy of Management Review* 45(1):196–214.

Garud, R., and Rappa, M.A. 1994. A socio-cognitive model of technology evolution: The case of cochlear implants. *Organisation Science* 5(3):344–362.

Gasson, S. 2004. The management of distributed organizational knowledge. In *Proceedings of the 37th Hawaii international conference on systems sciences*, ed. R.J. Sprague. IEEE Computer Society Press.

Gehrke, J. 2000. Tutorial on Knowledge Discovery and Data Mining, Pacific-Asia Conference on Advances in Knowledge Discovery and Data Mining, PAKDD 2000, Kyoto.

Giddens, A. 1979. *Central problems in social theory: Action, structure and contradiction in social analysis*. London: Macmillan.

Giddens, A. 1984. *The constitution of society: Outline of the theory of structuration*. San Francisco: University of California Press.

Giddens, A. 1991. *Modernity and self-identify*. Cambridge: Polity Press.

Gilbert, W. 1991. Towards a paradigm shift in biology. *Nature* 349:99.

Gödel, K. 1931. Über formal unentscheidbare Sätze der Principia Mathematica und verwandter Systeme. *Monatshefte für Mathematik und Physik* 38:173–98.

Grant, J., and Mackenzie, M. 2010, February 18. Ghost in the machine. *Financial Times.*

Grant, R. 1996a. Prospering in dynamically-competitive environments: Organizational capability as knowledge integration. *Organizational Science* 7(4):375–387.

Grant, R. 1996b. Toward a knowledge based theory of firm. *Strategic Management Journal* 17:109–122.

Grossman, R.L., Kamath, C., Kumar, V., and Namburu, R.R. 2001. *Data mining for scientific and engineering applications*. Boston: Kluwer Academic Publishers.

Gruber, T.R. 1993. A translation approach to portable ontology specifications. *Knowledge Acquisition*, 5(2):199–206.

Gu, J.F. 2001. Meta-synthesis knowledge system, *Research Report* AMSS-2001-7. Institute of Systems Science, Academy of Mathematics and Systems Sciences, Chinese Academy of Sciences, January 18.

Gu, J.F. 2004. How to synthesize experts opinions-building consensus from different perspectives. In *Proceedings of the 5th International Symposium on Knowledge and Systems Sciences*, 291–295. JAIST. Japan, November 10–12.

Gu, J.F. 2006. *Expert mining for discussing the social complex problems*. Presented at 6th International Workshop on Meta-Synthesis and Complex Systems (MCS2006). Beijing, September 22–25.

Gu, J.F. 2008. *Metasynthesis knowledge system: Basics and practice*. Presented at International Workshop on Knowledge Integration. Dalian, China, March 10.

Gu, J.F., Liu, Y.J., and Song, W.Q. 2007. A scientific discussion test on some social harmony problems. In *Proceedings of the 51st meeting of the International Society for the Systems Sciences (ISSS2007)*. Tokyo, August 5–10.

Gu, J.F., Song, W.Q., and Liu, Y.J. 2007. System, knowledge and traditional Chinese medicine. In *Proceedings of the 51st meeting of the International Society for the Systems Sciences (ISSS2007)*. Tokyo, August 5–10.

Gu, J.F., Song, W.Q., Zhu, Z.X., Gao, R., and Liu, Y.J. 2008. Expert mining and TCM knowledge. In *9th International symposium on knowledge and systems sciences (KSS2008)*. Guangzhou, China, December 11–13.

Gu, J.F., Song, W.Q., Zhu, Z.X., and Liu, Y.J. 2009. Expert mining and its applications. In *Proceedings of international conference on engineering and computational mathematics (ECM2009)*. Hong Kong, May 27.

Gu, J.F., and Tang, X.J. 2003. A test on meta-synthesis system approach to forecasting the GDP growth rate in china. In *Proceedings of 47th annual conference of the international society for the systems sciences*, R093.

Gu, J.F., and Tang, X.J. 2005. Meta-synthesis approach to complex system modeling. *European Journal of Operational Research* 166(3):597–614.

Gu, J.F., and Tang, X.J. 2006. *Wuli-Shili-Renli system approach: Theory and applications.* Shanghai: Shanghai Science and Technology, Education Publisher.

Gu, J.F., and Tang, X.J. 2007. Meta-synthesis systems approach and knowledge science. *International Journal of Information Technology and Decision Making*, 6(3):491–508.

Gu, J.F., Tang, X.J., and Zhu, Z.X. 2007. Survey on Wuli-Shili-Renli system approach. *Journal of Transportation Systems Engineering and Information Technology* 7(6):51–60.

Gu, J.F., Wang, H.C., and Tang, X.J. 2007. *Meta-synthesis method system and systematology research.* Beijing: Science Press.

Gu, J.F., and Zhu, Z.C. 1995. The Wuli-Shili-Renli approach (WSR): An Oriental system methodology. In *System methodology: Possibilities for cross-cultural learning and integration*, ed G. Midgley and J. Wilby, 31–40. Scarborough, UK: University of Hull.

Habermas, J. 1972. *Knowledge and human interests* (J. Shapiro, Trans.). London: Heinemann.

Han, J., Cheng, H., Xin, D., and Yan, X. 2007. Frequent pattern mining: Current status and future directions. *Data Mining and Knowledge Discovery* 15:55–86.

Han, J., and Kamber, M. 2006. *Data mining: Concepts and techniques.* San Francisco: Morgan Kaufmann.

Hand, D., Mannila, H., and Smyth, P. 2001. *Principles of data mining.* Cambridge, MA: MIT Press.

Handzic, M. 2004. *Knowledge management: Through the technology glass.* Toh Tuck Link, Singapore: World Scientific Publishing Co. Pte. Ltd.

Hastie, T., Tibshinari, R., and Friedman, J. 2008. *The elements of statistical learning: Data mining, inference and prediction* (2d ed.). New York: Springer.

Heidegger, M. 1954. Die Technik und die Kehre. In *Vorträge und aufsätze,* ed. M. Heidegger. Pfullingen: Günther Neske Verlag.

Heidegger, M. 1957. *Der Satz vom Grund.* Stuttgart: Nachfolger.

Heisenberg, W. 1927. Über den anschaulichen Inhalt der quantentheoretischen Kinematik und Mechanik. *Zeitschrift für Physik* 43:172–198.

Ho, T.B., Kawasaki, S., and Granat, J. 2007. Knowledge acquisition by machine learning and data mining. In *Creative Environments: Issues of Creativity Support for the Knowledge Civilization Age*, ed. A. P. Wierzbicki and Y. Nakamori, 69–91. Berlin: Springer-Verlag.

Ho, T.B., Kawasaki, S., Takabayashi, K., and Nguyen, C.H. 2007. Integration of learning methods, medical literature and expert inspection in medical data mining. *IEICE Trans. Information and Systems*, E90-D, 10, 1574–1581.

Ho, T.B., Nguyen, C.H., Kawasaki, S., Le, S.Q., and Takabayashi, K. 2007. Temporal relations extraction in mining hepatitis data. *Journal of New Generation Computing* 25(3):247–262.

Ho, T.B., and Nguyen, D.D. 2003. Chance discovery and learning minority classes. *Journal of New Generation Computing* 21(2):147–160.

Ho, T.B., Nguyen, T.D., Kawasaki, S., Le, S.Q., Nguyen, D.D., Yokoi, H., and Takabayashi, K. 2003. Mining hepatitis data with temporal abstraction. In *Proceedings of ACM international conference on knowledge discovery and data mining* KDD-03, 369–377.

Ho, T.B., Nguyen, T.D., Shimodaira, H., and Kimura, M. 2003. A knowledge discovery system with support for model selection and visualization. *Applied Intelligence* 19(1–2):125–141.

Ho, T.B., Nguyen, T.P., and Tran, T.N. 2007. Study of protein–protein interactions from multiple data sources. In *Advances in data warehousing and mining*, ed. T. David, 280–307. IGC Publishers.

Hofmann, T. 1990. Probabilistic latent semantic analysis. In *Proceedings of the 15th conference on uncertainty in artificial intelligence*. Stockholm, Sweden, July 30–August 1.

Hotho, A., and Numberger, A. 2005. A brief survey of text mining. *Journal for Computational Linguistics and Language Technology* 20(11):19–62.

Huntington, S.P. 1993. The clash of civilization? *Foreign Affairs* 72(3):22–49.

Huntington, S.P. 1996. *The clash of civilization and the remaking of world order*. New York: Simon and Schuster.

Ideker, T., and Sharan, R. 2008. Protein network in disease. *Genome Research* 18:644–652.

Izenman, A.J. 2008. *Modern multivariate statistical techniques: Regression, classification, and manifold learning*. New York: Springer.

Jackson, M.C. 2003. *Systems thinking: Creative holism for managers*. Chichester, UK: John Wiley and Sons.

Jackson, M.C., and Keys, P. 1984. Towards a system of systems methodologies. *Journal of the Operational Research Society* 35:473–486.

Jarzabkowski, P. 2004. Strategy as practice: Recursiveness, adaptation, and practices-in-use. *Organisation Studies* 25(4):529–560.

Jin, Z.Y. 2002. Soft technology—The essential of innovation. http://Millenium-project.org/millenium/Beijing-0702.pdf

Jin, Z.Y. 2005. *Global technological change: From hard technology to soft technology*. Bristol, UK: Intellect.

Johnson, B., Lorenz, E., and Lundvall, B.A. 2002. Why all this fuss about codified and tacit knowledge? *Industrial and Corporate Change* 11:245–262.

Jordan, M. 1998. *Learning in graphical models*. Cambridge, MA: MIT Press.

Jurafsky, D., and Martin, J.H. 2008. *Speech and language processing* (2d ed.). Upper Saddle River, NJ: Prentice Hall.

Kamath, C. 2009. *Scientific data mining: A practical perspective*. Philadelphia, PA: Siam.

Kant, I. 1781. *Kritik der reinen Vernunft*. Translated as *Krytyka czystego rozumu*. (Warsaw: PWN,1957).

Kaplan, R.S., and Norton, D.P. 2005. The balanced scorecard: Measures that drive performance. *Harvard Business Review* July–August, 172–180.

Kawano, S., and Nakamori, Y. 2000. Environment knowledge management using the framework model. In *Proceedings of international symposium on knowledge and systems sciences*, 111–116, September 25–27, JAIST, Japan.

Kawasaki, S., Nguyen, T.D., and Ho, T.B. 2003. Temporal abstraction for long-term changed tests in the hepatitis domain. *Journal of Advanced Computational Intelligence & Intelligent Informatics* 17(3):348–354.

Kennedy, D., and Norman, C. 2005. What don't we know? *Science* 309(5731): 75–102.

Kleinberg, J.M. 1999. Authoritative sources in a hyperlinked environment. *Journal of the Association for Computing Machinery* 46:604–632.

Kołakowski, L. 1988. *Metaphysical Horror.* Oxford: Blackwell.

Kosala, R., and Blockeel, H. 2000. Web mining research: A survey. *SIGKDD Explorations* 1(2):1–15.

Kriefgel, H.P., Borgwardt, K.M., Kroger, P., Pryakhin, A., Schubert, M., and Zimek, A. 2007. Future trends in data mining. *Data Mining and Knowledge Discovery* 15:87–97.

Król, Z. 2007. The emergence of new concepts in science. In *Creative environments: Issues of creativity support for the knowledge civilization age,* ed. A.P Wierzbicki, and Y. Nakamori, 417–444. Berlin: Springer-Verlag.

Kuhn, T.S. 1962. *The structure of scientific revolutions.* Chicago, IL: Chicago University Press.

Kunifuji, S., Kawaji, T., Onabuta, T., Hirata, T., Sakamoto, R., and Kato, N. 2004. Creativity support systems in JAIST. In *Proceedings of JAIST forum 2004: Technology creation based on knowledge science,* 56–58.

Lacroix, Z., and Critchlow, T., eds. 2003. *Bioinformatics: Managing scientific data.* San Francisco: Morgan Kaufmann.

Langley, P., and Simon, H.A. 1995. Applications of machine learning and rule induction. *Communications of the ACM* 38(11):54–64.

Latour, B. 1987. *Science in action.* Milton Keynes: Open University Press.

Laudan, R., ed. (1984) *The nature of technological knowledge: Are models of scientific change relevant?* Dordrecht: Reidel.

Lavrak, N., Motoda, H., Fawcett, T., Langley, P., and Adriaans, P. 2004. Lessons learned from data mining applications and collaborative problem solving. *Machine Learning* 57:13–34.

Le, M.H., Ho, T.B., and Nakamori, Y. 2005. Detecting emerging trends from scientific corpora. *International Journal of Knowledge and Systems Science* 2(2):53–59.

Le, N.T., Ho, T.B., and Tran, D.H. 2009. Characterizing nucleosome dynamics from genomic and epigenetic information using rule induction learning. *BMC Genomics* 10(Suppl.3):S27.

Leonard-Barton, D. 1992. The factory as a learning laboratory. *Sloan Management Review* 34(1):23–38.

Lewandowski, A., and Wierzbicki, A.P., eds. 1989. *Aspiration based decision support systems.* Berlin: Springer-Verlag.

Linstone, H.A. 1984. *Multiple perspectives for decision making.* New York: North-Holland.

Linstone, H.A., and Zhu, Z.C. 2000. Towards synergy in multiperspective management: An American-Chinese case. *Human Systems Management* 19:25–37.

Liu, B. 2007. *Web data mining,* Berlin: Springer-Verlag.

Liu, H., and Motoda, H. 1998. *Feature extraction, construction and selection: A data mining perpective.* Boston: Kluwer Academic Publishers.

Liu, Y.J., Niu, W.Y., and Gu, J.F. 2007. Exploring computational scheme of complex problem solving based on meta-synthesis approach. In *Lecture notes in computer science* 4490:9–17.

Locke, J. 1690/2005. An essay concerning human understanding. In *Knowledge: Critical concept,* ed. N.R. Stehri and R. Grundmann. Routledge.

Łukasiewicz, J. 1911. O wartościach logicznyh (On logical values). *Ruch Filozoficzny* I:50–59.

Ma, T., and Nakamori, Y. 2004. Roadmapping and *i*-System for supporting scientific research. In *Proceedings of the 5th International Symposium on Knowledge and Systems Sciences*, 77–80, JAIST, Japan, November 10–12.

Maier, R. 2007. *Knowledge management systems*. Berlin: Springer-Verlag.

Maier, R., and Remus, U. 2007. Integrating knowledge management services-strategy and infrastructure. In *Knowledge management and business strategies: Theoretical frameworks and empirical research*, ed. E.S. Abou-Zeid. Hershey.

Manning, C.D., Raghavan, P., and Schutze, H. 2008. *Introduction to information retrieval*. Cambridge, UK: Cambridge University Press.

Manning, C.D., and Schutze, H. 2001. *Foundations of Statistical Natural Language Processing*. Cambridge, MA: MIT Press.

Marakas, G.M. 2003. *Decision support systems in 21st century*, 2nd edition. New Jersey: Prentice Hall.

Mestrovic, S.G. 1998. *Anthony Giddens: The last modernist*. Oxford: Routledge.

Midgley, G. 2000. *Systems intervention: Philosophy, methodology and practice*. New York: Kluwer/Plenum.

Midgley, G. 2004. Systems thinking for the 21st century. *International Journal of Knowledge and Systems Sciences* 1(1):63–69.

Mintzberg, H. 2007. Productivity is killing American enterprise. *Harvard Business Review* July–August, 25.

Mitchell, T. 1997. *Machine learning*. New York: McGraw-Hill.

Motoda, H., Ho, T.B., Washio, T., Yada, K., Yoshida, T., and Ohara, K. 2005. Active mining for structured data. *Journal of Japanese Society for Artificial Intelligence* 20(2):172–179.

Motycka, A. 1998. *Nauka a nieświadomość*. Translated as *Science and unconscious*, in Polish. Wroclaw: Leopoldinum.

Mulej, M. 2007. Systems theory—A world view and/or a methodology aimed at requisite holism/realism of human's thinking, decisions and action. *Systems Research and Behavioral Science* 24(3):347–357.

Nahapiet, J., and Ghoshal, S. 1998. Social capital, intellectual capital, and the organizational advantage. *Academy of Management Review* 23(2):242–266.

Nakamori, Y. 2000. Knowledge management system toward sustainable society. In *Proceedings of the 1st international symposium on knowledge and system sciences*, 57–64. September 25–27, JAIST, Japan.

Nakamori, Y. 2003. Systems methodology and mathematical models for knowledge management. *Journal of Systems Science and Systems Engineering* 12(1):49–72.

Nakamori, Y. 2008. A methodology for knowledge synthesis. At *A seminar of meta-synthesis and complex systems in Chinese academy of sciences*, December 5.

Nakamori, Y. 2009. Methodology for knowledge synthesis. In *Proceedings of 20th international conference (MCDM 2009): Cutting-edge research topics on multiple criteria decision making*, 311–317. Chengdu, China, June 21–26.

Nakamori, Y., and Wierzbicki, A.P. 2010. Systems approach to knowledge synthesis. *International Journal of Knowledge and Systems Science* 1(1):1–13.

Nakamori, Y., and Zhu, Z.C. 2004. Exploring a sociologist understanding for the *i*-System. *International Journal of Knowledge and Systems Sciences* 1(1):1–8.

National Institute of Science and Technology Policy (NISTEP). 1988. A survey on present situation and future trend of r&d of series of soft science and technology, Japanese Financial Group Legal Person, March.

National Institute of Science and Technology Policy (NISTEP). 1989. A survey on present situation and future trend of r&d of series of soft science and technology, Japanese Financial Group Legal Person, March.

Nguyen, D.D., Ho, T.B., and Kawasaki, S. 2006. Knowledge visualization in hepatitis study. In *Proceedings of Asia Pacific symposium on information visualization (APVIS 2006)*, 59–62. February 1–3, Tokyo.

Nguyen, T.P., and Ho, T.B. 2007. A semi-supervised learning approach to disease gene prediction. In *Proceedings of 2007 IEEE International Conference on BioInformation and BioMedicine (BIBM)*, Silicon Valley, November 2–4, 423–428.

Nguyen, T.P., and Ho, T.B. 2008. An integrative domain-based approach to predicting protein–protein interactions. *Journal of Bioinformatics and Computational Biology* 6(6):1115–1132.

Nguyen, T.C., Sugiyama, A., Fujiwara, A., Mitani, T., and Dam, H.C. 2009. Density functional study of Pt_4 cluster adsorbed on a carbon nanotube support. *Physical Review B* 79(23), 235417.

Nonaka, I. 1991. The knowledge-creating company. *Harvard Business Review,* November–December, 96–104.

Nonaka, I. 1994. A dynamic theory of organizational knowledge creation. *Organizational Science* 5(1):14–37.

Nonaka, I., and Konno, N. 1998. The concept of "ba": Building a foundation for knowledge creation. *California Management Review* 40(3):40–54.

Nonaka, I., and Takeuchi, H. 1995. *The knowledge-creating company: How Japanese companies create the dynamics of innovation*. Oxford: Oxford University Press.

Nonaka, I., Toyama, R., and Hirata, T. 2008. *Managing flow: A process theory of the knowledge-based firm*. New York: Palgrave Macmillan.

Nonaka, I., Toyama, R., and Konno, N. 2000. SECI, ba and leadership: A unified model of dynamic knowledge creation. *Long Range Planning* 33:5–34.

Pawlak, Z. 1991. *Rough sets—Theoretical aspects of reasoning about data*. Dordrecht: Kluwer.

Pham, T.H., Clemente, J., Satou, K., and Ho, T.B. 2005. Computational discovery of transcriptional regulatory rules. *Bioinformatics* 21(Supp.2):101–107.

Pham, T.H., and Ho, T.B. 2007. A hyper-heuristic for descriptive rule induction. *International Journal of Data Warehousing and Mining* 3(1):54–66.

Pham, T.H., Satou, K., and Ho, T.B. 2005. Support vector machines for prediction and analysis of beta and gamma turns in proteins. *Journal of Bioinformatics and Computational Biology* 3(2):343–358.

Pham, T.H., Tran, D.H., Ho, T.B., Satou, K., and Valiente, G. 2005. Qualitatively predicting acetylation and methylation areas in dna sequences. *Genome Informatics 2005*, Yokohama, Universal Academic Press 15(2):3–11.

Plato. ca. 380 BC. *Dialogues*. Translated as *Verum* (Warszawa, 1993).

Polanyi, M. 1958. *Personal knowledge: Towards a post-critical philosophy*. London: Routledge and Kegan Paul.

Polanyi, M. 1966. *The tacit dimension*. London: Routledge and Kegan Paul.

Popper, K.R. 1934. *Logik der forschung*. Vienna: Julius Springer Verlag.

Popper, K.R. 1956. Three views concerning human knowledge. In *Contemporary British Philosophy, Third Series*, ed. W.H.D. Lewis. London: Allen and Unwin.

Popper, K.R. 1972. *Objective Knowledge*. Oxford, UK: Oxford University Press.

Powell, J.H., and Swart, J. 2005. This is what the fuss is about: A systemic modelling for organizational knowing. *Journal of Knowledge Management* 9(2):45–58.

Pyle, D. 1999. *Data preparation for data mining.* San Francisco: Morgan Kaufmann.

Qian, X.S., Yu, J.Y., and Dai, R.W. 1990. A new discipline of science—The study of open complex giant system and its methodology. *Nature Magazine* 13:3–10.

Quine, W.V. 1953/1964. Two dogmas of empiricism. In *Philosophy of Mathematics,* eds. P. Benacerraf and H. Putnam. Englewood Cliffs, NJ: Prentice-Hall.

Ramakrishnan, R., and Grama, A.Y. 2001. Mining scientific data. In *Advances in Computers,* ed. M. Zelkowitz, 55:119–169. San Diego: Academic Press.

Rashidi, H.H., and Buehler, L.K. 2000. *Bioinformatics basics: Applications in biological sciences and medicine.* Boca Raton, FL: CRC Press.

Reich, R. 2010. Recovery depends on Main Street. *Financial Times,* March 24.

Roberts, J. 2004. *The modern firm.* Oxford, UK: Oxford University Press.

Rorty, R. 1980. *Philosophy and the mirror of nature.* Princeton, NJ: Princeton University Press.

Ruggles, R. 1998. The state of the notion: Knowledge management in practice. *California Management Review* 40(3):80–89.

Ryoke, M., Yamashita, Y., Hori, K., and Nakamori, Y. 2007. Knowledge discovery of interview survey on fresh food management. *International Journal of Knowledge and Systems Sciences* 4(1):31–34.

Sawaragi, Y, Naito M, and Nakamori, Y. 1990. Shinayakana systems approach in environment management. In *Proceedings of the 11th world congress on automatic control,* Vol. 5:511–516. Pergamon Press, Tallinn, USSR, August 13–17.

Schölkopf, B., and Smola, A. 2001. *Learning with kernels: Support vector machines, regularization, optimization, and beyond.* Cambridge, MA: MIT Press.

Schölkopf, B., Tsuda, K., and Vert, J.P. 2004. *Kernel methods in computation biology.* Cambridge, MA: MIT Press.

Schreiber, G., Akkermans, H., Anjewierden, A., de Hoog, R., Shadbolt, N., Van de Velde, W., et al. 2000. *Knowledge engineering and management: The common KADS methodology.* Cambridge, MA: MIT Press.

Scott, W.R. 1995. *Institutions and organisations.* Thousand Oaks, CA: Sage.

Sewell, W.H., Jr. 1992. A theory of structure: Duality, agency, and transformation. *American Journal of Sociology* 98(1):1–29.

Shapiro, S.C., ed. 1992. *Encyclopedia of artificial intelligence* (2d ed.). New York: John Wiley and Sons.

Simon, H.A. 1957. *Models of man.* New York: Macmillan.

Snow, C.P. 1960. *The two cultures.* Cambridge, UK: Cambridge University Press.

Soft Series Science and Technology Investigation Committee. 1990. Japan Science and Technology Policy Office of Science and Technology Agency.

Springer, S., and Deutsch, G. 1981. *Left Brain–Right Brain.* New York: Freeman.

Swanson, D.R., and Smalheiser, N.R. 1997. An interactive system for finding complementary literatures: A stimulus to scientific discovery. *Artificial Intelligence* 91:183–203.

Tang, X.J., and Gu, J.F. 2001. WSR analysis to the development of an enterprise management software project. In *Proceedings of 45th annual conference of the international society for the systems science* (Paper No. 01-093). Asilomar, CA, July 8–13.

Tang, X.J., and Liu, Y.J. 2002. A prototype environment for group argumentation. In *Proceedings of the third international symposium on knowledge and systems sciences,* 252–256. Shanghai, August 7–8.

Tang, X.J., Zhang, N., and Wang, Z. 2007. Exploration of TCM masters knowledge mining. In *Computational science—Proceedings of ICCS2007, Part IV,* Y. ed. Shi et al. Also in *Lecture Notes in Computer Science* 4490, 35–42. Berlin: Springer-Verlag.

Teece, D.J. 2008. From the management of R&D to knowledge management—Some contributions of Ikujiro Nonaka to the field of strategic management. In *Managing flow: A process theory of the knowledge-based firm,* ed. I. Nonaka, I. Tonyma, and T. Hirata, pp. ix–xvii. Basingstoke, UK: Palgrave Macmillan.

Tran, D.H., Satou, K., and Ho, T.B. 2008. Finding microRNA regulatory modules in human genome using rule induction. *Journal BMC Bioinformatics* 9(Supp 11):1–10.

Tukey, J.W. 1977. *Exploratory data analysis.* Reading, MA: Addison-Wesley.

Tushman, M.L., and Anderson, P. 1986. Technological discontinuities and organizational environments. *Administrative Science Quarterly* 31:439–465.

Vollmer, G. 1984. Mesocosm and objective knowledge: On problems solved by evolutionary epistemology. In *Concepts and approaches in evolutionary epistemology,* ed. F.M. Wuketits and D. Reidel. Dordrecht: D. Reidel Publishing Company.

Walker, M.P., Brakefield, T., Morgan, A., Hobson, J., and Stickgold, R. 2003. Practise with sleep makes perfect: Sleep dependent motor skill learning. *Neuron* 35(1):205–211.

Wang, J.T.L., Zaki, M., Toivonen, H.N.N., and Shasha, D. 2004. *Data mining in bioinformatics.* Berlin: Springer-Verlag.

Wang, Z.T. 2004. Knowledge systems engineering: A new discipline for knowledge management and enabling. *International Journal of Knowledge and Systems Sciences* 1(1):9–16.

Weiss, S., Indurkhya, N., Zhang, T., and Damerau, F.J. 2006. *Text mining: Predictive methods for analyzing unstructured data.* Berlin: Springer-Verlag.

Wierzbicki, A.P. 1997. On the role of intuition in decision making and some ways of multicriteria aid of intuition. *Multiple Criteria Decision Making* 6:65–78.

Wierzbicki, A.P. 2007. Technology and change: The role of technology in knowledge civilization. In *Creative environments—Issues of creativity support for the knowledge civilization age,* ed. A.P. Wierzbicki and Y. Nakamori, 385–416, Berlin: Springer-Verlag.

Wierzbicki, A.P., Kameoka, A., and Nakamori, Y. 2008. The new era of knowledge civilization and its episteme. In *Futurology—The challenges of the XXI century,* ed. A. Kukliński and K. Pawłowski, 45–82. Pruszków: Rewasz.

Wierzbicki, A.P., and Nakamori, Y. 2006. *Creative space: Models of creative processes for the knowledge civilization age.* Berlin: Springer-Verlag.

Wierzbicki, A.P., and Nakamori, Y., eds. 2007a. *Creative environments: Issues of creativity support for the knowledge civilization age.* Berlin: Springer-Verlag.

Wierzbicki, A.P., and Nakamori, Y. 2007b. *Testing knowledge creation theories.* Presented at IFIP-TC7 Conference. Krakow, Poland, July 23–27.

Wierzbicki, A.P., Zhu, Z.C., and Nakamori, Y. 2006. A new role of systems science: Informed systems approach. In *Creative space: Models of creative processes for the knowledge civilization age,* eds. A.P. Wierzbicki and Y. Nakamori, 161–215. Berlin: Springer-Verlag.

Wilson, T.D. 2002. The nonsense of "knowledge management." *Information Research* 8(1). Available at: http://informationr.net/ir/8-1/paper144.html.

Wittgenstein, L. 1922. *Tractatus logico-philosophicus.* Cambridge, UK: Cambridge University Press.

Wittgenstein, L. 1969. *On certainty*. In *On Certainty*, eds. G.E.M Anscombe and G.H. von Wright. Oxford: Blackwell.

Wu, X.D., Kumar, V., Quinlan, R.J., Ghosh, J., Yang, Q., Motoda, H., et al. 2008. Top 10 algorithms in data mining, *Knowledge Information Systems* 14:1–37.

Yamashita, Y., and Nakamori, Y. 2007. Knowledge integration methodology for designing a knowledge base of technology development in traditional craft industry. In *Proceedings of the 2007 IEEE international conference on systems, man, and cybernetics*, 332–337. October 7–10, Montreal, Canada.

Yang, Q., and Wu, X.D. 2006. 10 challenging problems in data mining research. *International Journal of Information Technology & Decision Making* 5(4):597–604.

Young, L.F. 1983. Computer support for creative decision-making: Right-brained DSS. In *Processes and tools for decision support*, ed. H.G. Sol. Amsterdam: North-Holland.

Zadeh, L. 1965. Fuzzy sets. *Information and Control* 8:338–353.

Zhu, Z.C. 1998. Conscious mind, forgetting mind: Two approaches in multimethodology. *Systems Practice and Action Research* 11(6):669–690.

Zhu, Z.C. 1999. The practice of multimodal approaches, the challenge of cross-cultural communication, and the search for responses. *Human Relations* 52(5):579–607.

Zhu, Z.C. 2000. Dealing with a differentiated whole: The philosophy of the WSR approach. *Systemic Practice and Action Research* 13(1):21–57.

Zhu, Z.C. 2008 Knowledge, knowing, knower: What is to be managed and does it matter? *Knowledge Management Research and Practice* 6:112–123.

Index

T - #0140 - 101024 - C0 - 234/156/10 [12] - CB - 9781439838365 - Gloss Lamination